BEDFORD COLLEGE EDITIONS

Henry James

Daisy Miller

WILLA CATHER, *MY ÁNTONIA*

Edited by Guy Reynolds,
University of Nebraska-Lincoln

KATE CHOPIN, *THE AWAKENING*

Edited by Sharon M. Harris,
University of Connecticut

NATHANIEL HAWTHORNE,
THE SCARLET LETTER

Edited by Susan S. Williams,
The Ohio State University

HENRY JAMES, *DAISY MILLER*

Edited by William Merrill Decker,
Oklahoma State University

HERMAN MELVILLE, *BENITO CERENO*

Edited by Wyn Kelley,
Massachusetts Institute of Technology

SUSANNA ROWSON,
CHARLOTTE TEMPLE

Edited by Pattie Cowell,
Colorado State University

HARRIET BEECHER STOWE,
UNCLE TOM'S CABIN

Edited by Stephen Railton,
University of Virginia

MARK TWAIN, *ADVENTURES OF
HUCKLEBERRY FINN*

Edited by Gregg Camfield,
University of California, Merced

BEDFORD COLLEGE EDITIONS

Henry James

Daisy Miller

Edited by William Merrill Decker
Oklahoma State University

Bedford/St. Martin's
BOSTON • NEW YORK

For Bedford/St. Martin's

SENIOR EXECUTIVE EDITOR: Stephen A. Scipione
PRODUCTION SUPERVISOR: Victoria Sharoyan
MARKETING MANAGER: Stacey Propps
ASSOCIATE EDITOR: Alyssa Demirjian
PROJECT MANAGEMENT: DeMasi Design and Publishing Services
PERMISSIONS MANAGER: Kalina K. Ingham
TEXT DESIGN: Judith Arisman/Arisman Design Studio
COVER DESIGN: Donna Lee Dennison
COVER ART: *Morning Walk* by John Singer Sargent
COMPOSITION: Jeff Miller Book Design
PRINTING AND BINDING: RR Donnelley and Sons

PRESIDENT, BEDFORD/ST. MARTIN'S: Denise B. Wydra
PRESIDENTS, MACMILLAN HIGHER EDUCATION: Joan E. Feinberg
    and Tom Scotty
EDITOR IN CHIEF: Karen S. Henry
DIRECTOR OF MARKETING: Karen R. Soeltz
PRODUCTION DIRECTOR: Susan W. Brown
ASSOCIATE PRODUCTION DIRECTOR: Elise S. Kaiser
MANAGER, PUBLISHING SERVICES: Andrea Cava

Manufactured in the United States of America.

7 6 5 4 3 2
f e d c b a

For information, write: Bedford/St. Martin's, 75 Arlington Street, Boston, MA 02116
    (617-399-4000)

ISBN 978-1-4576-0770-7

Preface

ABOUT THE SERIES

THE BEDFORD COLLEGE EDITIONS reprint enduring literary works in an informative, readable, and affordable format. The text of each work is lightly but helpfully annotated. Prepared by eminent scholars and teachers, the editorial matter in each volume includes a chronology of the life of the author; an illustrated introduction to the contexts and major issues of the text in its time and ours; an annotated bibliography for further reading (contexts, criticism, and Internet resources); and a concise glossary of literary terms.

ABOUT THIS VOLUME

Daisy Miller has served generations of readers as a gateway to the works of Henry James, a prolific and ever inventive author to whom one may return again and again for renewed pleasure and satisfaction. In this short narrative of James's early middle period one finds nearly all of his signature themes: confrontations between American naïveté and European sophistication; the claims of aspiring youth against the complacence and corruption of age; contrasts between new and old money; courtship that challenges the powerful constraints of nationality and class; and, finally, education in the ways of the world that comes at a sobering price. This edition restores *Daisy Miller* to the freshness of its initial appearance in 1878, a time of great social and geographic mobility in the United States and confusion as to its post-Civil War identity. Late-nineteenth-century America was a land of contradictions: caught up in a series of boom and bust cycles, labor unrest, racial and class injustice, the country also witnessed a relentless industrial expansion, massive creation of wealth, the formation of a new leisured class, and the emergence of what we may think of as a uniquely privileged American adolescence – conditions, in short, that launch Daisy Miller on European tour. The Introduction contextualizes the narrative among these trends and addresses the ways in which James positions his reader among such currents of social change. A chronology of the life of Henry James precedes the annotated text; suggestions for further study and research follow it.

ACKNOWLEDGMENTS

I thank Susan Belasco and Linck Johnson, editors of *The Bedford Anthology of American Literature*, for inviting me to undertake this project. Bedford College Editions series editor, Steve Scipione, has provided wonderful guidance from start to finish. I am indebted to others who helped at Bedford, including Alyssa Demirjian, who prepared the manuscript for production, and Andrea Cava and Linda DeMasi who steered it through the production process. My research assistant, Jason Tillis, was indispensable to the preparation of the text. The students of my spring semester 2011 English 4300 (Exotic Destinations) class brought their characteristic enthusiasm to our reading of *Daisy Miller* and provided valuable counsel on the matter of annotations. Jeffrey Walker and Art Redding read the Introduction and made their usual excellent suggestions. Thanks are also due to Carol Moder, head of the English Department at Oklahoma State University, for research support, and Daniel Crutcher, OSU Institute of Teaching and Learning Excellence, for assistance in digitalizing the illustrations. Finally, I thank my colleague and spouse, Elizabeth Grubgeld, for conversation about this project.

Contents

Chronology: The Life of Henry James

1843   Birth of Henry James on April 15 in New York City. He is the second child of Henry James and Mary Robertson Walsh James, and younger brother of William James (1842-1910), who will become a distinguished psychologist, philosopher, and author of *The Varieties of Religious Experience*.

1843-1845   First residence abroad. Henry and William along with their parents and aunt Catharine Walsh reside in England and France. Henry James Sr. experiences a psychological episode he later terms his "vastation," as a result of which he becomes a follower of the doctrines of philosopher and mystic Emanuel Swedenborg.

1845   Family returns to the United States. They divide their time between New York City and the Albany residence of Henry's grandfather, William James, a Protestant Irish immigrant

	who has made a fortune speculating in upstate New York real estate. Garth Wilkinson James is born.
1846	Robertson James is born.
1847	Family establishes itself in lower Manhattan and over the next few years their house becomes a meeting place for American and British literary figures, including Ralph Waldo Emerson, Horace Greeley, William Cullen Bryant, Bronson Alcott, and William Makepeace Thackeray.
1848	Alice James is born. She will acquire a literary reputation for her posthumously published diary and letters.
1855-1859	Second residence abroad. Motivated by a desire to find schooling superior to the private instruction available to his children in New York City, Henry James Sr. moves the family to London, Geneva, and Paris in search of adequate tutors and schools. Returning to the United States, the family settles in Newport, Rhode Island.
1859-1862	Third residence abroad. Henry James Sr. again settles the family in Geneva where William attends the Geneva Academy (predecessor of the University of Geneva) and Henry is enrolled for a short time in a secondary school that emphasizes science and mathematics, for which he has little aptitude. During summer 1860 Henry studies German in Bonn. He returns with his family to the United States the following September. Henry befriends his orphaned cousin May (Minnie) Temple, on whom Isabel Archer (*The Portrait of a Lady*) and, to a lesser degree, Daisy Miller are modeled. In an effort to combat a barn fire, Henry sustains an unspecified injury that disqualifies him for military service.
1862	Henry enrolls in Harvard Law School, while brothers Garth and Robertson enlist in the Union Army. Breaking off his legal studies, James commits himself to a literary vocation.
1864-1865	Begins to publish his first stories. Contributes reviews and travel sketches to *The Nation* and *The Atlantic.*
1869	First solo tour of Europe. Meets various prominent figures including Dante Gabriel Rossetti, William Morris, Charles Darwin, George Eliot, and Leslie Stephen, who will become editor of *Cornhill Magazine* in 1871. First visit to Italy. While in Rome he learns of cousin Minnie Temple's death.
1870	Returns to Cambridge, Massachusetts, where his family is now permanently settled. First novel, *Watch and Ward*, is serialized in *The Atlantic Monthly.*

1872-1874	Tours England and the continent with Aunt Kate (Catharine Walsh) and Alice. Contributes travel sketches to *The Nation.*
1875	Following a year in New York City, James moves to Paris and thus begins long-term European residency. Forms strong friendship with Turgenev, and regularly attends Flaubert's Sunday Evenings where he also meets Maupassant and Zola. *Roderick Hudson* is serialized in *The Atlantic Monthly.*
1877	Publishes *The American.*
1878	*Daisy Miller* appears in the June and July issues of *Cornhill Magazine* and is promptly pirated by New York and Boston newspapers. James acquires international celebrity. *The Europeans* is published later in the year as is "An International Episode."
1879	James publishes *Confidence* and *Hawthorne*, a work combining criticism and biography. An authorized *Daisy Miller* appears in the United States as a pamphlet in Harper Brothers' Half-Hour Series.
1881	*Washington Square* and *The Portrait of a Lady* appear to great acclaim.
1882-1883	James returns to the United States. In short order, his mother, father, and brother Wilkinson die. *Daisy Miller* appears in *The Atlantic Monthly* as a play with a happy ending.
1884	Publishes his highly influential essay "The Art of Fiction."
1886	*The Bostonians* and *The Princess Casamassima.* Both works draw mixed reviews.
1888	*The Reverberator* and *The Aspern Papers.*
1890	*The Tragic Muse.*
1892	Alice James dies.
1893	*The Real Thing and Other Tales.*
1895	James makes a serious effort to write for the theater. *Guy Domville* fails spectacularly and he returns to prose fiction. *Terminations*, a collection of tales, appears.
1896	*The Spoils of Poynton* and *Embarrassments*, a collection that includes "The Figure in the Carpet."
1897	*What Maisie Knew.*
1898	*The Turn of the Screw.*
1899	*The Awkward Age.*
1901	*The Sacred Fount.*

1902	*The Wings of the Dove.* This is the first of three novels that mark the culmination of James's mastery as a novelist.
1903	*The Ambassadors.*
1904	*The Golden Bowl.*
1905	Publishes *English Hours*, a collection of sketches written over several decades. Returns a final time to the United States and embarks on an extensive rail tour of the country, visiting the South and the West Coast as well as the familiar Northeast.
1907	Publishes *The American Scene*, a travel narrative recounting his return to what for James was a radically transformed twentieth-century America.
1908	Publishes *Italian Hours*. Like *English Hours*, this volume collects sketches written over several decades.
1913	*A Small Boy and Others*, the first of two autobiographical narratives.
1914	*Notes of a Son and Brother.* This is his second autobiographical narrative and the last work James would see through to completion. Shares in the deep distress caused by the onset of World War I.
1915	James suffers a series of strokes in December.
1916	James dies on February 28.

An Introduction to *Daisy Miller*

THE PUBLICATION OF *Daisy Miller* in 1878 marked Henry James's arrival as a literary professional and advanced his celebrity on both sides of the Atlantic. Having served a remarkably prolific probation (in 1877 he published his third novel, *The American*), he garnered international fame with this sleek novella depicting the misadventures of an American family on European tour. Once in print, *Daisy Miller*'s popularity was all but assured given its smooth integration of fresh and compelling themes: foreign travel, sexual taboo, contrasts between Old and New Worlds, and conflict between good and evil masquerading as respective opposites. Chronicling the escapades of a beautiful girl from upstate New York, *Daisy Miller* situates an "exotic" American in equally "exotic" European settings and gives a new and erotic twist to the classic cross-cultural encounter. It presents Daisy as an emerging type of American young woman but also as a girl whose "reputation" (or, in plain English, her presumed sexual history) is subject to perpetual if inconclusive speculation. Readers today might easily imagine the ardent sensation such portraiture should produce.

For in 1878, sex – or, more accurately, the suggestion of it – exerted a scandalous appeal, just as it does in our own day, and the novella's whispered publication backstory did much to fuel that suggestion. *Daisy Miller: A Study* first appeared in the June and July 1878 issues of the London-based *Cornhill Magazine.* Initially James had offered the story to the American *Lippincott's Magazine*; only after meeting rejection at home did he seek the English venue. In an era that predated the rule of international copyright, however, British and American publishers routinely raided one another: within weeks a pirated *Daisy Miller* circulated in Boston and New York. The fact that *Daisy Miller* was spurned by an American editor, proceeded to win favor in England, and only then found an American public through the back door of unauthorized printing, gave it the air of a text that would not be suppressed. The *Lippincott* editor never explained his decision to decline *Daisy Miller*, but decades later, savoring the novella's risqué history, James claimed he was told by "a friend" that the tale had been judged in Philadelphia to constitute "an outrage on American girlhood" ("Preface" 1269). Leon Edel may be right to insist that the *succès de scandale* attributed to *Daisy Miller* has been overplayed, but this little tour de force, republished in 1879 under the author's supervision in Harper Brothers' Half-Hour pamphlet series, enjoyed a vogue nourished by controversy (*Conquest* 308-09). Soon after its first stateside circulation, William Dean Howells remarked that James had "waked up all the women with his Daisy Miller, the intention of which they misconceived, and there has been a vast discussion in which nobody felt very deeply, and everybody talked very loudly. The thing went so far that society almost divided itself into Daisy Millerites and anti-Daisy Millerites" (230-31). The hubbub extended well beyond the tale's actual audience. Like Rip Van Winkle, Poe's raven, and (somewhat later) Huckleberry Finn, Daisy achieved the status of a pop-culture icon, a point of reference for the reading and nonreading public alike. "Daisy Miller hats" found their way to the milliner's shelves. A certain kind of American girl was called "a Daisy Miller." The tale appeared in translation and Virginia W. Johnson published *An English Daisy Miller.* The charm of the character and her eponymous tale far exceeded James's expectations.

Freely based on incidents that had animated gossip among the American expatriate colony in Rome and about which James had heard second-hand from his friend Alice Bartlett, *Daisy Miller* draws upon the full range of the novelist's knowledge of European and American conventions and personalities. While the story is not exactly autobiographical, one can see how it resonates with James's unusual life experience. Son of the theologian Henry James Sr., and younger brother of William James, psychologist and pragmatist philosopher to be, James was born in 1843 in New York City where his well-heeled and eccentric family resided off and on through his first twelve years. Before he was twenty, the household – which also included his formidable mother, Mary Walsh James, and in time three younger siblings, brothers Wilkinson and Robertson, and sister Alice James, who would win fame as a diarist – had moved a dozen times and completed three European residencies. While frequent displacement made it hard for these children to establish roots in any one place, the stimulating nature of any place their cerebral parents chose to lodge permitted the hyper-observant Henry to form an acquaintance with highly diverse locales. A lifelong student of personality (the brilliant and overbearing personalities of his family made this a condition of psychic survival), James was exposed to an astonishing range of human variation in his early years, and recurrently in his fiction some curious instance of individuality, often a character removed from an accustomed context, faces some life-defining decision or stumbles on a life-altering recognition. A portraitist of radiant and magnetic individuals, James was equally committed to elucidating the representative nature of any singular case. Although arguably "a very light young person," Daisy is one such radiant individual. She stands out from the crowd of American tourists but serves nonetheless as an exemplar of collective traits.

THE MOBILE AFFLUENT AMERICAN GIRL

As the novella's title suggests, Daisy commands the narrative front and center, but remains strategically ever beyond the purview of the narrator's limited omniscience. We never quite know her as she knows herself. Unlike the American expatriate Frederick Winterbourne, to whose hesitant thought and ambivalent reflex the reader has access, Daisy stands a little apart and dominates the story as someone who engrosses Winterbourne's baffled attention. The subtitle, "a study," introduces the idea that Daisy's appearance may belie her reality; it also underscores the fact that what we are given to know about her is generally conveyed by the observations of individuals who seldom see beyond what convention and prejudice prepare them to see. From beginning to end our perspective shadows that of Winterbourne, who watches, escorts, and comes very close to stalking Daisy,

Figure 1. Winterbourne's idea of Daisy Miller. Illustrated by Harry W. McVickar for the 1892 Harper and Brothers edition.

without entirely understanding what compels his attraction to the fresh young woman so clearly his inferior in class and so pathetically his junior in worldly experience. The subtitle highlights the surveillance to which Winterbourne and his fellow expatriates subject Daisy, but it also encourages readers to assess the presumption and consequences of that surveillance. Must Annie P. "Daisy" Miller be included in the roll call of fallen women in American literature – a roster featuring (among others) Charlotte Temple, Hester Prynne, Edna Pontellier, and Ántonia Shimerda? Far from convicting her of misconduct, to mention Daisy in such company extends our consideration of what "fallen" means in a squeamish culture that encourages citizens to fantasize the sexual forays of their neighbors. Readers today, like readers in 1878, must draw their own conclusions, interpreting Daisy in the light of the other characters' assessments, deciding where to confer benefit of the doubt, or whether doubt pertains to this case after all.

In the end, we may learn more about the student of Daisy than we do about Daisy herself, but it is important to recognize that for *Daisy Miller*'s author and first readers, whose social affiliations correspond far more with Winterbourne, Mrs. Costello, and Mrs. Walker than with the Millers, Daisy merits study because her behavior constitutes evidence that the world has changed. In 1878 Daisy is a new kind of person and her novelty is both demographic and literary. Demographically, she represents a young American female whose father's recently acquired wealth provides her with leisured alternatives to early marriage, farm work, or life as a mill hand or domestic (Kett 168-71). Like generations of middle-class American teenagers who have come of age since the end of World War II, but unlike all but a few young people in post-Civil War America, Daisy has opportunities to socialize, shop, and venture beyond the authority of her not-very-authoritarian parents. She might well strike us as a prophecy of affluent and prolonged adolescence. Literarily, she is absolutely a novelty: the creature of the "realist" tendency in post-Civil War fiction dedicated to examining a democratizing and rapidly evolving social order, one that generates novel forms of personhood that defy comprehension by the old class codes. The most prominent early representation of the blonde mainstream "American girl," Daisy serves as prototype of the beach movie ingénue and boy-crazy teen. The fact that we meet her on vacation is significant. As James had depicted Christopher Newman the year before in *The American*, and as he would portray Isabel Archer, heroine of *The Portrait of a Lady*, three years later, he presents Daisy not as she might be found at home in the small industrial hinterland city, but as one who has already crossed an ocean and national border or two – as someone, that is, wholly given to the era's unprecedented social and geographic mobility.

In the world of James's fiction, Daisy stands as perhaps the most naïve and vulnerable incarnation of a character he recurrently sought to model: the new democratic individual for whom no historical precedent exists, an individual who represents a radical break with European tradition and bears at best a remote kinship to the aristocratic circles of the American metropolitan centers (Boston, New York, Philadelphia). Christopher Newman, Isabel Archer, and Lambert Strether arise, like Daisy, from the republic's industrial interiors to present a profile whose significance transcends the individual case. How, James implicitly asks, to limn this new social phenomenon, this class of materially successful Americans who have acquired the resources to pursue amusement and meaning beyond their regional horizons? Again and again throughout his career, the answer is to portray them as tourists, travelers, pilgrims, and expatriates: the restless products of a progressive civilization whose success destabilizes everything that has come before. From the early tale "A Passionate Pilgrim" to the late novel *The Golden Bowl*, James examines his countrymen and women in the context of old, conservative, decaying worlds that cling to their vengeful hierarchies. Whether he is writing fiction or nonfiction, his work qualifies as travel literature in the broadest sense: narrative that not only depicts individuals sojourning in foreign lands but also delineates whole worlds in transition. In creating such literature James became a major exponent of a central theme of modernity.

NINETEENTH-CENTURY AMERICAN MOBILITY: TRAVELING IN CLASS

It is therefore fitting that James's arrival as a man of letters should take place in an expatriate setting, reflecting as it does the narrative of United States citizens arriving individually and en masse on European shores. In modest numbers Americans had crossed the Atlantic for business and pleasure from the colonial period forward. Through much of the nineteenth century, privileged young men commonly embarked on a postbaccalaureate "grand tour" before settling into the sedentary rounds of professional and family life. Men and women of artistic and literary calling established residencies in European capitals, as did small colonies of leisured Americans who could afford to live where and how they chose. James Fenimore Cooper, Washington Irving, Nathaniel Hawthorne, and Margaret Fuller all spent productive years living abroad, as did nearly every significant painter and sculptor of the early national period – John Singleton Copley, Gilbert Stuart, Benjamin West, Washington Allston, Horatio Greenough, to name a few. The novelist's father, Henry James Sr., inherited from his father, William James, a moderate fortune that allowed him to pursue a life of philosophical inquiry and to indulge his own nomadic inclinations. He accordingly installed his family in a series of European locales – London, Paris, Geneva, sites that deeply impressed the child Henry and to which he formed lasting homelike attachments. The novelist's early transatlantic residence not only exposed him to the cultures and languages of Europe but also to a wide spectrum of Americans – various in temperament, literary and artistic gifts, personal merit, and material means – who enjoyed the benefit of living among the historical centers of Western culture but who, in naturalizing themselves to England, France, Germany, and Italy, incurred the risk of alienating themselves from an America that continued to evolve in their absence.

Following the Civil War, Americans of old money and artistic aspiration were joined by upwardly mobile fellow citizens whose European excursions were facilitated by a general rise and distribution of wealth, steady advances in steamship technology, and a travel industry that had developed affordable package tours. During the first half of the century, two thousand to eight thousand Americans annually crossed the Atlantic to Europe; after the Civil War, the figure jumped to forty thousand (Withey 61, 156). The comic possibilities of Americans descending on Europe had been exploited as far back as the London episode of Benjamin Franklin's *Autobiography* (1793) and Washington Irving's *Sketchbook of Geoffrey Crayon* (1819). The theme would receive definitive treatment in Mark Twain's *The Innocents Abroad* (1869) and persist as a staple of American humor well into the next century. *National Lampoon's European Vacation* (1985) and Bill Bryson's *Neither Here Nor There: Travels in Europe* (1991) are well-known recent examples that reflect the increasingly common middle-class experience of family travel in Europe and the transformation of the grand tour into backpacking expeditions conducted on Spartan budgets. Directed primarily at domestic audiences, such narratives invite Americans to laugh at themselves and their European hosts. Implicitly they celebrate the U.S. citizen's global mobility and challenge the notion that some (the educated and wealthy) are more adept at such travel than are others. For Americans whose international travel has been motivated by a desire to distance themselves from mainstream American consumer culture, however, such humor has always had its limits.

Beginning with *The American*, James himself contributed to the comic tradition of Americans in Europe. In the novels of his middle and late periods – *The Portrait of a Lady, The Ambassadors, The Wings of the Dove, The Golden Bowl* – he explored both comic and tragic nuances inherent in the collision of New and Old Worlds. But as a young man embarked, in 1869, on his first solo tour, mortified by the hordes of Americans for whom European travel served chiefly to confirm the superiority of everything American, he saw very little humor indeed. Childhood residence in France, England, and Switzerland had worked an inevitable Europeanizing effect. He was fluent in French and Italian and adept at assimilating to local custom; no one could be better positioned to note the shortcomings of

Americans on their first and in many cases only tour. In the travel essays he contributed to *The Nation* (we might note in passing that the travel sketch genre only reinforced an American readership's burgeoning wanderlust) he makes reference to "one's detested fellow-pilgrim" (*Collected Travel Writings* 400). Writing to his mother in 1869, he appears totally unsympathetic with the lot of his culturally narrow countrymen and women: "Their ignorance – their stingy, defiant, grudging attitude towards everything European – their perpetual reference of all things to some American standard or precedent which exists only in their own unscrupulous windbags – and then our unhappy poverty of voice, of speech, and of physiognomy – these things glare at you hideously" (*Henry James Letters* I: 152). Eight years later, he would depict Christopher Newman, protagonist of *The American*, as a wayfarer who evinces nearly every vice a man of limited experience and unlimited arrogant means might exhibit, but whose core integrity and educable sensibility compensates for the poverty of his native culture. And a year after that, even as he presents the Millers as the most ludicrous of American tourists (certain *Daisy Miller* incidents would be right at home in a *National Lampoon* vacation film), he portrays their petty consumerism with a measure of pathos and manifests a qualified endorsement of such American traits as incite the laughter of European lackeys and wrath of American expatriates. For by then James had developed the capacity to see more than one side of the national character and had become acquainted with the limitations of an expatriate perspective that had lost contact with an American frame of reference. Aristocratic by temperament, constitutionally averse to mixing with the likes of the Millers, he could not repress the memory of his own family's rise. As a man of broad cross-cultural observations he understood that in an era of class and geographic mobility, everyone's social identity is in flux.

The provinciality of Daisy and her family and their innocence among the hazards of new wealth are topics on which James, himself the child of a comparatively recent affluence, was in fact qualified to speak. The Millers represent first-generation fortunes; while Mr. Miller remains in Schenectady supervising the unidentified enterprise that has made his family rich, his wife and two children embark on an extended European tour. For his part, James, although a native of New York City, spent part of his childhood in Albany, near neighbor of Schenectady, at the home of his grandfather, William James, an enterprising Scotts-Irish immigrant who arrived penniless but proceeded to build an American fortune from speculating in upstate New York real estate. For U.S. families one generation can make a big difference; whereas Albany, seat of his grandfather's rapid wealth making, figures in James's infancy and early childhood, so too does Manhattan with its promise of cosmopolitan life. Later, during his household's second and third sojourns in Europe, residence in Geneva furnished James with material from which to mold Daisy's perplexed halfhearted suitor, Winterbourne. But James himself was never so perplexed as the expatriate Winterbourne. Equipped with knowledge of the inland valleys, he authoritatively conveys Mrs. Miller's bewildered affect and the brutal *r*'s that characterize Randolph's regional accent. Having resided in Newport and seen the daughters of a rising industrialism adorn the fashionable resorts, he could readily visualize Daisy's wardrobe, facial mannerisms, and body language; he could imagine her phrases and could predict how such expression would be interpreted by young men unaccustomed to such performances. If, given the narrative point of view, the reader is prompted to experience a little of Winterbourne's befuddlement at the appearance of the Millers, the authorial intelligence that models Daisy and her family knows the demographics of this group very well.

Benefiting from this larger perspective, the reader is thus positioned to observe Winterbourne and to consider the lesson his experience offers him. Point of view in *Daisy Miller* is so anchored in the young man's perspective that a case could be made that he, and not Daisy, is the novella's principal character. For the narrative's core question concerns how one is supposed to relate to people of a lower social scale with whom one shares (beyond, of course, some portion of common humanity) a half-buried element of national identity that binds like a distant family connection. It is through Winterbourne's eyes that we first see Daisy and through his ears that we gather information about the girl and her family. Moreover, we are privy to his manner of processing this information – nearly all of it prejudiced in disfavor of the Millers – against his strong spontaneous attraction to the girl, largely but not entirely explained by her striking beauty, exquisite dress, and the sheer audacity of her self-possession: in sum, her American freshness and vulnerability. Every event in the story plays out with reference to Winterbourne as active or passive participant, and even when he is outwardly inactive, the story advances in accord with his preoccupation – his mulling over reports of Daisy in the unchaperoned company of handsome Italian men, his speculation as to the place in her life of the "beautiful Giovanelli." At the center of the narrative is Winterbourne's judgment of Daisy, the question, from his standpoint, of how she must be judged, as "simply a pretty girl from New York State" or as "an audacious, an unscrupulous young person," and the degree to which, after several attempts at definitive answers, he can afford to let the question go.

Figure 2. Winterbourne. Illustrated by Harry W. McVickar for the 1892 Harper and Brothers edition.

Compelled as we are to ponder Daisy through the filter of Winterbourne's subjectivity, we are nevertheless permitted an objective view of Winterbourne's interactions with and conjectures concerning her. As readers partnered with his perspective, we are set at a sufficient distance to see how Winterbourne establishes that perspective and can therefore consider his distinct limitations as we assess his readings of the American girl.

Since Winterbourne provides our point of departure in ascertaining Daisy, it is well to take stock of what we actually know about him. Except for our inside psychological view during their rapidly evolving friendship (call it a courtship, perhaps a "flirtship"), we have actually little to go on. We know less biographically about Winterbourne than we do about Daisy. Given the explanation of his residence in Geneva as an "old attachment for the little metropolis of Calvinism," it might be supposed that he has Puritan New England antecedents. We can assume that he has enough family money of the "old" variety to live abroad and lead the career of a perpetual student. To the degree that the little we know about Winterbourne confirms his standing among the respectable classes, however, the narrative deceptively encourages us to dispense with background checks – to accept him as a normative "one of us." We can see for ourselves that he is amiable and knowledgeable, that he has polished if painfully inflexible manners, and that, as far as family loyalty is concerned, he is solicitous of his Aunt Costello, far more so than are her own children. Yet there is additional and, so the narrator concedes, unconfirmed dirt in Winterbourne's dossier: that he is content to postpone marriage and a settled existence while he entertains the attentions of older, married European women. There is the suggestion that Winterbourne, with near-perfect discretion, sustains elements of corruption in his personal life. Daisy attempts to flush into the open what the narrator merely insinuates concerning Winterbourne's amatory arrangements in Geneva, although her intuition senses another woman, not an immoral attachment. But the point is well taken: anyone's privacy can be the object of speculation, and despite our "omniscient" access to Winterbourne there are details we cannot know.

Winterbourne's social identity and personal ethics are important to consider inasmuch as *Daisy Miller* engages the reader in vicarious acts of social judgment for which the young man serves as proxy. Although we are discouraged from identifying too closely with him, judicious as he often seems in comparison with his bigoted aunt or the vengeful Mrs. Walker, the story implicitly proposes that our level of knowledge and sophistication approximates his. James can safely assume that we will share some element of Winterbourne's dismay over Daisy's indiscretions: for the narrative to function, the reader's grasp of social convention must absolutely transcend that of Daisy, her mother, and Randolph. In spite of their millions, the Millers are strategically framed as "our" social inferiors, although we may suspect all along that such framing sets us up for the story's admonitory turn. But once the narrative has established our superiority to the Millers (by no means a difficult task: even the most sympathetic reader is likely to smile at Mrs. Miller's gaucheries), we are entrapped, so to speak, in committing vicarious acts of snobbery, and such complicity can only call into question the reader's own experience, taste, education, and social status. Even as James compels readers to look with disdain on the Millers, he highlights the ethical implications of judging and dismissing our human likeness on what are essentially class-determined criteria. We miss an important dimension of the tale if we ignore the author-reader dynamic, the narrative's manipulation of our class-status reflex and incitement to invidious reflection. Given James's recognition that social identity is extremely fluid and that literary marketplaces are marked but not bound by class, nation, or language, it therefore makes sense to consider who in 1878 he expects to read *Daisy Miller* and what common social denominators unite those he visualizes as constituting his audience. His attempt to place the novella in *Lippincott's* followed by his successful bid to publish it in *Cornhill* provide one kind of evidence, as both periodicals appealed to educated upper-middle-class to upper-class readers. *Lippincott's* and *Cornhill* both represent a culture to which the Millers have yet to attain. But we can also identify in-text evidence with respect to James's expectations, and it is here especially that we see him probe issues of class identity as it relates both to his characters and his readers.

The opening sentences indicate that James envisions his readers as a mobile and leisured lot. "At the little town of Vevey, in Switzerland, there is a particularly comfortable hotel. There are, indeed, many hotels; for the entertainment of tourists is the business of the place, which, as many travelers will remember, is seated upon the edge of a remarkably blue lake – a lake that it behooves every tourist to visit." Not every reader "will remember" this particular lake, but James can assume that his audience possesses a familiarity with travel and resort stays. He proceeds to describe the range of hotels that line the shore from " 'the grand hotel' of the newest fashion" to "the little Swiss *pension* of an elder day" catering to an international clientele among whom, "in the month of June, American travelers are extremely numerous." The language of this paragraph evokes the rapid development of a formerly exclusive summer retreat into a broadly commercial vacation site, patronized by newly moneyed classes who are buying their way into erstwhile aristocratic preserves. Readers in 1878 were prompted thus to locate themselves somewhere along this privileged spectrum. After providing a wide-angle glimpse of Lake Geneva's resort row, the narrator returns to the "particularly comfortable hotel" mentioned in the first sentence, namely the "Trois Couronnes," an establishment "distinguished from many of its upstart neighbours by an air both of luxury and of maturity." Such qualities, the narrator suggests, may remind American travelers of Ocean House (Newport) and Congress Hall

Figure 3. Vevey: Hôtel des Trois Couronnes.

(Saratoga), old-style aristocratic hotels catering to the young democracy's elite. In one of the story's initial reversals of expectation, the Trois Couronnes, the most exclusive hotel in Vevey, patronized by Mrs. Costello, turns out to be the lodging of the upstart Millers who might be thought to prefer a hotel "with a chalk-white front, a hundred balconies, and a dozen flags flying from its roof" – a hotel at their level of luxury and maturity. Anyone who has traveled and lodged according to a sense of station will be aware of this incongruity. Nouveau riche as readers with this sort of experience themselves may be, James makes it easy for them to regard the Millers as rank gate-crashers.

Entering what James lays out as the familiarly exotic world of *Daisy Miller,* readers are thus coaxed to self-identify as more or less seasoned travelers of an elite class standing. Where one stays makes a difference, but so too what one does and with what foreknowledge one embraces the travel occasion. Beyond the superficial significance of lodging, *Daisy Miller* unfolds amid a geography deeply shaded by the romantic and generally tragic bearing of European history. The gross ignorance of the Millers begs the question of what individual readers can demonstrate by way of a presumably superior knowledge. They may know hotels and have a rudimentary grasp of castles, but beyond the safety of the illuminated tourist path, James sets readers adrift in an increasingly perilous terrain – perilous, certainly, beyond the reckoning of either Daisy or Winterbourne. Despite its colonization by arriving hordes and full-service hotels, Europe is not yet homogenized in the manner of a Newport or Saratoga Springs. For James if not for his reader, each particular European locale evokes historical narratives against which the story of Americans on tour will always seem lightweight. In the end mere American class distinctions may not count for much. The tragedies of high- and lowborn Americans seem destined to remain of a pathetic cast.

TOURIST ITINERARIES AND CULTURAL GEOGRAPHIES

Geneva and Vevey, situated on Lake Geneva (Lac Léman) in predominantly French-speaking Switzerland, harbor deep associations with the Reformation, Enlightenment, and Romantic eras. James alludes to these associations more and less explicitly. A longtime resident of Geneva, Winterbourne is said to have "an old attachment for the little metropolis of Calvinism." This need not mean that he subscribes to the severe theology of the Protestant reformer John Calvin (1509-1564) whose doctrines developed in opposition to the grand bureaucracy of the Roman Catholic Church and provided a basis for New England Congregationalism. It may, however, confirm personal tendencies suggested by his frosty name and self-acknowledged stiffness of manner, unmitigated by whatever liaisons he has formed with older and only nominally married European women, and indicate a propensity to imagine the innate depravity lurking beneath a show of innocence. Conspicuously, James does not identify Geneva as the city of Jean-Jacques Rousseau (1712-1778), a seminal Romantic philosopher and novelist who set *Julie, or the New Heloise* (1761), his massive epistolary novel about the illicit love of a teacher (Saint-Preux) for his pupil (Julie), in Vevey. Only a remote analogy exists in Winterbourne's relationship to Daisy and readers who know *Julie* will note the significant contrast. Geneva and environs are also associated with Voltaire, Gibbon, Madame de Staël, Shelley, and Byron, who collectively mark the site as a participant in the turbulence of Enlightenment and Romantic Europe, as well as a city that from the seventeenth century forward could claim a seriously academic culture. Henry James Sr., who vigorously rejected the Calvinism of his father the Presbyterian Irish immigrant, twice located the family in Geneva so that his children might enroll in the city's reputedly progressive schools. Winterbourne is said to have "been put to school there as a boy, and he had afterwards

Figure 4. Lake Geneva.

gone to college there," but we are never encouraged to think of him as a
student with a particular vocation, much less a scholar of divinity. Amid
the international vacation atmosphere of Vevey on the east side of the
lake, in a mood superficially more consistent with Rousseau, Winterbourne
feels less bound by formal convention, and thus is eager to speak with
Daisy in the absence of a supervising elder and to propose a visit to the
Château de Chillon. Although he enjoys recounting his unmonitored conversation with the pretty girl to Mrs. Costello, who predictably disapproves
of such behavior, he himself is never quite comfortable in departing from
Geneva protocols. The castle date promises to be a romantic excursion and
as a long-term resident and perennial student, Winterbourne is well versed
in Chillon's history, or at least in the episode involving François Bonivard,
a monk who refused to renounce his beliefs, and whose defiance in the
face of incarceration and suffering had been celebrated in two of Byron's
poems, "The Sonnet of Chillon" and "The Prisoner of Chillon." But Winterbourne is neither Bonivard nor Byron, much less Rousseau or Saint-Preux.
He is a conventionally learned Victorian American for whom Europe exists
as a sequence of theme parks.

To Daisy, the Château de Chillon is simply "that castle," a pasteboard
image without history; to her mother, it is not even worth visiting as it

does not appear on the castle master list and, as she says, speaking like a true consumer, "we only want to see the principal ones." The novella presents the Millers as the sort of American tourists on whom the opportunities of European travel are lost; when the scene shifts to the Eternal City that impression is only reinforced. In Mrs. Walker's drawing room, responding to Winterbourne's question "how she was pleased with Rome," Mrs. Miller is candid: "I must say I am disappointed. . . . We had heard so much about it; I suppose we had heard too much. But we couldn't help that. We had been led to expect something different." (The passage reads like a page from *The Innocents Abroad*; all that remains is for Mrs. Miller to complain of being "swindled.") That "something different" is never specified, but it might have been something other than the transitional rough-edged Rome of the late 1870s, the energized center of a newly unified Italy and no longer the seat of the Papal States, now reduced to the circumscribed enclave of Vatican City. The government of King Victor Emanuel II had initiated programs to convert Rome from a ruinous if picturesque ancient and medieval city to a modern, secular, national capital, so that the Millers would have arrived at a moment when excavation projects were unearthing monuments in and around the Forum and an up-to-date sanitary system was still a work in progress. Neither a student of the past nor of history-in-the-making, Daisy is heartily pleased with Rome. "It's a great deal nicer than I thought," she tells Winterbourne. "I thought it would be fearfully quiet; I was sure it would be awfully poky. I was sure we should be going round all the time with one of those dreadful old men that explain about the pictures and things. But we only had about a week of that, and now I'm enjoying myself." Daisy explains that her enjoyment derives from "the society," international and "extremely select," and it is evident to Winterbourne that, as his aunt had reported, this girl with the pretty American teeth has become the magnet for a bevy of Italian fortune hunters.

The Millers' obliviousness to the significance of Rome is particularly noteworthy. Since the advent of the grand tour, Rome with its pagan and Christian heritage, its republican, imperial, and ecclesiastical past, its showcase of Renaissance art, has typically figured as the itinerary's culmination for the children of privilege trained in the classics. As a participant in the grand tour tradition, James himself experienced Rome as ultimate destination during his 1869 solo excursion: "At last – for the first time – I live," he reports to his parents. "It beats everything: it leaves the Rome of your fancy – your education – nowhere." The letter rhapsodizes at length in this vein: "I went reeling and moaning thro' the streets, in a fever of enjoyment. In the course of four or five hours I traversed almost the whole

Figure 5. Mr. Giovanelli. Illustrated by Harry W. McVickar for the 1892 Harper and Brothers edition.

of Rome and got a glimpse of everything – the Forum, the Coliseum (stupendissimo!), the Pantheon, the Capitol, St. Peter's, the Column of Trajan, the Castle of St. Angelo – all the Piazzas and ruins and monuments. The effect is something indescribable. For the first time I know what the picturesque is" (*Henry James Letters* I: 308). The Rome James visited in 1869 was in the last days of papal authority, a decrepit site of unexhumed glories that his friend and fellow grand tour alumnus Henry Adams recalled years later as "sorcery": "the lights and shadows were still medieval, and medieval Rome was alive; the shadows breathed and glowed, full of soft forms felt by lost senses. No sand-blast of science had yet skinned off the epidermis of history, thought, and feeling. The pictures were uncleaned, the churches unrestored, the ruins unexcavated." Although James and Adams similarly confirm that nothing in one's education quite prepares

American youth for Rome, both betray the influence of *The Marble Faun* (1850), Nathaniel Hawthorne's tale of Anglo-American artists who come under the spell of the city's sorcery in spite of its "nervous and unwholesome atmosphere" (36), who explore Rome from the Catacombs to the Pincio Gardens, and who, risking the famous fever, pay "the inevitable visit by moonlight" to the Coliseum, all the while "exalting themselves with raptures that were Byron's, not their own" (155). But Adams and James counter Hawthorne by insisting that their Roman exaltations were particularly those of American youth.

The Rome of *Daisy Miller* has begun to enter a more modern world but Adams's characterization would have still held true with respect to its powers of seduction. Rome may have been "a gospel of anarchy and vice; the last place under the sun for educating the young; yet it was, by common consent, the only spot that the young – of either sex and every race – passionately, perversely, wickedly loved" (802). Daisy may prove susceptible to little beyond the generically romantic appeal of the European scene, and is incapable of taking an interest in "pictures and things," but at some level she registers the emotion Adams evokes, and feels that her Roman adventure is not complete without the attentions of Italian men and the "inevitable" visit to the Coliseum by moonlight, preferably in the company of an indigenous beau. Emulating the Americans of *The Marble Faun*, Winterbourne conjures the spirit of Byron: drawn to the moonlit Coliseum on a solitary nocturnal walk, he recites lines from *Manfred* before he notices the presence of Daisy and Giovanelli. But unlike Kenyon and Hilda, Winterbourne has trouble approaching anything with rapture, Byron's or his own. He exhibits no such intoxication with Europe as James expresses in his letters home. His sole source of emotional stimulus is Daisy. But he is, as Daisy frequently reminds him, "stiff," habitually repressing the springs of affection, denying the intensity of his attraction to this stunning American girl.

METAPHYSICS AND ETHICS OF CLASS DISTINCTION

In *Daisy Miller*, two Americans participate in a kind of courtship fostered by a vacation context, one that most likely could not have occurred at home. It is ironic that Americans must leave the theoretically egalitarian United States and mingle in historically class-stratified Europe to form relationships across American social barriers. But the international encounter of U.S. citizens separated from one another by region, class, and ethnicity is a recurrent motif in travel narratives – one need look no further than Hemingway's *The Sun Also Rises* or the travel essays James Baldwin includes in *Notes of a Native Son* for examples. An odd match from the very start, Winterbourne and Daisy form a bond neither can quite define. From their first meeting there persists a mutual attraction and answerability rooted in common national origin.

So much of the analysis of Daisy – whether the narrator's, Winterbourne's, Mrs. Costello's, or Mrs. Walker's – concerns her deficiencies of class, education, and discretion that we may easily lose sight of those aspects of American identity that commend Daisy to Winterbourne's attention. From the moment the Millers first appear Winterbourne begins to recognize his estrangement from his native land. Contemplating the antics of Randolph, shipped against his will overseas, he wonders "if he himself had been like this in his infancy, for he had been brought to Europe at about this age." Winterbourne perceives that expatriate life has produced in him a forgetfulness with regard to the realities of American life. At the vision of Daisy "dressed in white muslin, with a hundred frills and flounces, and knots of pale-colored ribbon," he thinks, "How pretty they are!" He perceives Daisy as the representative of a tantalizing and for him unattainable incarnation of American womanhood, at once alien and familiar, and his exclamatory reflection expresses his sense of the worlds that divide them. In the scene that follows in the garden of the Trois Couronnes, he makes awkward attempts to navigate such social space as should normally (for him) discourage contact and he is astonished to discover that space so readily traversed. He finds that with Daisy it is only too easy to strike up conversation. For a Winterbourne naturalized to the constraints of bourgeois Europe, such simplicity is itself a source of complication.

If some shared yet unnamable commonality draws Winterbourne to the Millers, it is precisely their "commonness" with which Mrs. Costello begins and ends her reproach. She warns her nephew not to "meddle with little American girls that are uncultivated, as you call them. You have lived too long out of the country. You will be sure to make some great mistake. You are too innocent." Responding later to Winterbourne's protest that "they are very ignorant – very innocent only" and his insistence that "they are not bad," she makes what for her is a definitive pronouncement: "They are hopelessly vulgar. . . . Whether or no being hopelessly vulgar is being 'bad' is a question for the metaphysicians. They are bad enough to dislike, at any rate; and for this short life that is quite enough." The socially exclusive Mrs. Costello succeeds in exempting herself from such metaphysical and ethical questions, but Winterbourne for the time being cannot take that position, nor can a serious reading leave those questions unaddressed.

Beneath the comedy of manners that arises from the encounter of old and new American wealth, the moral implications of judging others (a theme James inherits from Hawthorne) and doing so across class lines occupy the narrative from start to finish. Winterbourne knows better than to suspect Daisy of serious indiscretion, yet when he momentarily convinces himself that Daisy is disreputable he feels the relief of one who has sunk too much in a risky investment and is resigned to see it devalued. The scene in which Winterbourne stumbles on Daisy and Giovanelli in the Coliseum (the quick-eyed Daisy perceives the flatfooted Winterbourne before he can make his retreat) merits the reader's close attention, for this is the moment when Winterbourne stands morally as well as visually exposed. Temporarily at least, his faith in Daisy's virtue collapses: he is prey to such cynicism as afflicts and destroys Hawthorne's Goodman Brown.

But at no point does James treat the human folly of judging others in sermonic mode. For the reader whose class-zealous complicity James has sought to engage, there are comic as well as moral implications in our proclivity to invidious observation. "Vulgarity" in other words has entertainment value. Whether to distract from the metaphysics of such judgment or to press the issue more keenly, James enlists his audience in the guilty pleasure of laughing at social ineptitude. Some of the funniest moments of *Daisy Miller* occur when the representatives of old and new wealth converse across what for Mrs. Costello and (increasingly) Mrs. Walker is the great unbridgeable divide. Appearing before Mrs. Walker, who has invited the Millers to her party out of a sense of national civility and a waning hope that Daisy can be rescued from her scandalous tendencies, Mrs. Miller lamely apologizes for her daughter's delayed arrival.

> "She got dressed on purpose before dinner. But she's got a friend of hers there; that gentleman – the Italian – that she wanted to bring. They've got going at the piano; it seems as if they couldn't leave off. Mr. Giovanelli sings splendidly. But I guess they'll come before very long," concluded Mrs. Miller hopefully.

Her hostess responds concisely, her tartness barely concealed by her good breeding, but nuance is wasted on Mrs. Miller:

> "I'm sorry she should come – in that way," said Mrs. Walker.

> "Well, I told her that there was no use in her getting dressed before dinner if she was going to wait three hours," responded Daisy's mamma. "I didn't see the use of her putting on such a dress as that to sit round with Mr. Giovanelli."

Mrs. Walker's one line refers to the whole manner of Daisy's conduct and the scandal of Mrs. Miller leaving a teenaged daughter unsupervised with a foreign suitor of doubtful credentials, whereas for Mrs. Miller, whom Mrs. Walker has already described as an "imbecile," the only thing curious about Daisy's behavior concerns her decision to dress before dinner. "This is most horrible!" Mrs. Walker confides to Winterbourne just after this exchange.

Daisy's conversation can at times rival the inanity of her mother's, as when she prattles about the pretty dress she plans to wear to Mrs. Walker's party and when she asks permission to bring along her "intimate" Italian friend. But she has a quickness that allows her to match wits with Mrs. Walker and Winterbourne; if James prompts us to laugh at social ineptitude, he also presents upper-class stuffiness to comic effect. Daisy recurrently answers Winterbourne's pompous locutions with ridicule. Accompanying her as she defiantly strolls to the Pincian Gardens in pursuit of Giovanelli, Winterbourne proclaims that "I certainly shall not help you to find him."

"Then I shall find him without you," cried Miss Daisy.

"You certainly won't leave me!" cried Winterbourne.

She burst into her little laugh. "Are you afraid you'll get lost – or run over? But there's Giovanelli, leaning against that tree. He's staring at the women in the carriages: did you ever see anything so cool?"

Daisy's sparring with Mrs. Walker is equally spirited but here the comedy begins to take a more serious turn. Daisy scores often and cheaply and crows in her evident triumph, but socially the stakes are high and the game more dangerous than she can reckon.

"Do get in and drive with me!" said Mrs. Walker.

"That would be charming, but it's so enchanting just as I am!" and Daisy gave a brilliant glance at the gentlemen on either side of her.

"It may be enchanting, dear child, but it is not the custom here," urged Mrs. Walker, leaning forward in her victoria, with her hands devoutly clasped.

"Well, it ought to be, then!" said Daisy. "If I didn't walk I should expire."

"You should walk with your mother, dear," cried the lady from
Geneva, losing patience.

"With my mother dear!" exclaimed the young girl. Winterbourne
saw that she scented interference. "My mother never walked ten
steps in her life. And then, you know," she added with a laugh,
"I am more than five years old."

"You are old enough to be more reasonable. You are old enough,
dear Miss Miller, to be talked about."

Daisy looked at Mrs. Walker, smiling intensely. "Talked about?
What do you mean?"

"Come into my carriage, and I will tell you."

At this point a chagrined Daisy understands that this talk concerns her
sexual availability. Still, under pressure she demonstrates political skill:
sensing Winterbourne's supreme discomfort, she deflects this assault by
probing the alignment between Mrs. Walker and Winterbourne and assess-
ing the relative force of female and male authority.

"Does Mr. Winterbourne think," she asked slowly, smiling,
throwing back her head, and glancing at him from head to foot,
"that — to save my reputation — I ought to get into the carriage?"

Thus challenged, the young man who made bold to flirt with Daisy at Vevey
assumes the role of enforcer of social convention, although not without a
blush of embarrassment at Daisy's mention of "reputation," code word for
all that might be speculated of her life as an unchaste young woman. What
after all had been his intentions? Predictably he opines, "I think you
should get into the carriage."

Daisy gave a violent laugh. "I never heard anything so stiff! If this
is improper, Mrs. Walker," she pursued, "then I am all improper,
and you must give me up. Good-by; I hope you'll have a lovely ride!"

Readers must decide for themselves the value of Daisy's momentary
verbal victories, her assertion of a vernacular Emersonian self-reliance
and healthy egotism against the small-minded, "poky" customs of the
country. It is difficult not to admire her fidelity to her own "improper" self,
her declaration of intuitive feminist autonomy. She is a true if ever naïve
empiricist. In response to Winterbourne's asseverations about local conventions and in riposte to his limp explanation of why he has not come
round to see her, she exclaims, "I don't believe it!" She believes only what

Figure 6. Mrs. Walker. Illustrated by Harry W. McVickar for the 1892 Harper and Brothers edition.

she sees and understands at a glance. Christopher Newman, protagonist of *The American*, likewise frequently exclaims, "I don't believe it!" In both it bespeaks a mind that must know something directly and on its own terms. Daisy's words cut through a language of clouded refinement with what to readers of our own day seems like commonsense lucidity, but the price she pays is being "talked about": made an object of hostile and abusive discussion. Is she prepared for the ostracism this must entail? Again, we never enjoy direct access to Daisy's thought, but we are prompted to read the inner life by her involuntary facial expressions – she colors, she turns pale. Such moments coincide with Winterbourne's confirmations that she is being spoken of in ways that touch upon her sexuality and culminate in the moment in which Winterbourne tells Daisy that she can henceforth expect the expatriate community's "cold shoulder." But in all instances she just as rapidly recovers her composure, affecting a blithe acceptance of consequences. She is determined to have her fun and hold her ground and her words come fast when she is challenged. "I don't care," affirms Daisy in extremity, "whether I have Roman fever or not!" She has come to Rome with a set of puerile agenda. As she expresses herself in her most pregnant witticism of all: "We are going to stay all winter – if we don't die of the fever; and I guess we'll stay then."

Daisy captures the Holy Grail of tourist experience, to see the Coliseum by moonlight. Having spent little time familiarizing herself with Roman history and culture ("pictures and things"), it might be argued that her evening in the Coliseum reduces to fulfilling the checklist in a program of "vulgar" thrill seeking. As well, it might be argued that the Millers' European itinerary, their lodging in the most expensive hotels, and their appearance in extravagant clothes ("no," remarks Mrs. Costello to her nephew, marveling over Daisy's fine taste, "you don't know how well she dresses") is a textbook example of what Thorstein Veblen termed "conspicuous consumption," more specifically the "vicarious consumption" of a rich man's wife and children (77). But can the old-wealth Americans be said to have any higher motive for sojourning in Rome? In an 1873 letter to his mother written during his second visit to the city, James characterizes the expatriate colony as "without relations with the place, or much serious appreciation of it" (*Henry James Letters* I: 331). Such a comment would seem to apply exactly to the condition of Mrs. Costello and Mrs. Walker and at least in part to Winterbourne. If that is the case, why are they there?

It is a question to consider among the larger contexts of American social and geographical mobility in the nineteenth century. The narrative of westward migration – Europe to America, East Coast to the continental interiors – is associated with liberation from the European past and reinvention of the possibilities of life at both an individual and civic level, but what about the narrative of "return" to Europe? Does it imply a rejection of distinctly American manners, attitudes, and popular culture, all of which Daisy embodies? Does it involve nostalgia for the very social hierarchies Americans have traditionally prided themselves in rejecting? Can Winterbourne, Mrs. Costello, Mrs. Walker, and the Millers explain why they have crossed the Atlantic? For the self-made Christopher Newman of *The*

Figure 7. Coliseum. Illustrated by Harry W. McVickar for the 1892 Harper and Brothers edition.

American, the European excursion implements a very explicit agenda – to purchase a life of luxury and distinction that formerly one possessed only as a birthright – but except for Daisy, none of the Americans in *Daisy Miller* seems comparably purpose driven. If the old-wealth Americans reject the power of popular culture, do the Millers, with Daisy leading the charge, represent an evangelical movement to liberate Europe from its "poky" ways? Can any of these Americans anticipate how, in the course of this experience, they will change, or what transformations they have undergone as a result of an extended residence? Can they go home again and, if so, on what terms? Such questions, seldom asked much less answered in our era of much more accessible and casual international travel, pertain nevertheless to anyone's experience of crossing borders.

Works Cited

Adams, Henry. *Democracy, Esther, Mont Saint Michel and Chartres, The Education of Henry Adams, Poems.* Ed. Ernest Samuels and Jayne N. Samuels. New York: Library of America, 1983. Print.

Edel, Leon. *Henry James: The Untried Years, 1843-1870.* Philadelphia: Lippincott, 1953. Print.

———. *Henry James: The Conquest of London, 1870-1881.* Philadelphia: Lippincott, 1962. Print.

Hawthorne, Nathaniel. *The Centenary Edition of the Works of Nathaniel Hawthorne. Volume IV: The Marble Faun: or, The Romance of Monte Beni.* Ed. William Charvat et al. Columbus: Ohio State UP, 1968. Print.

Howells, William Dean. *The Selected Letters of William Dean Howells, 1873-1881.* Ed. Christoph K. Lohmann and Jerry Herron. Boston: Twayne, 1979. Print.

James, Henry. *Henry James Letters.* Vol. I, 1843-1875. Ed. Leon Edel. Cambridge: Belknap P of Harvard UP, 1974. Print.

———. *Collected Travel Writing: The Continent: A Little Tour in France, Italian Hours, Other Travels.* Ed. Richard Howard. New York: Library of America, 1993. Print.

———. "Preface to 'Daisy Miller' &c." In *Henry James: Literary Criticism: French Writers; Other European Writers; The Prefaces to the New York Edition.* Ed. Leon Edel and Mark Wilson. New York: Library of America, 1984.

Kett, Joseph F. *Rites of Passage: Adolescence in America, 1790 to the Present.* New York: Basic, 1977.

Veblen, Thorstein. *The Theory of the Leisure Class: An Economic Study of Institutions.* New York: Modern Library, 1931.

Withey, Lynne. *Grand Tours and Cook's Tours: A History of Leisure Travel, 1750 to 1915.* New York: Morrow, 1997.

A Note on the Text

Daisy Miller was first published in the June and July 1878 issues of *Cornhill Magazine*, a British monthly (1860-1975) originally edited by William Makepeace Thackeray. This edition reproduces the original *Cornhill* text. In 1879, the novella was reissued in Harper Brothers' Half-Hour pamphlet series. The 1879 Harper edition is nearly identical to the *Cornhill* text. *Daisy Miller* was destined to appear in two additional incarnations: as a play (1883) featuring a happy ending, which the *Atlantic Monthly* published in three installments and which James Osgood published in book form in 1884, and as the significantly rewritten tale James included in the *New York Edition of Henry James* (1907-1909). See Philip Horne, "Henry James at Work: The Question of Our Texts," for a detailed discussion of the *Daisy Miller* variants.

Daisy Miller
A Study in Two Parts

Henry James

Part I.

AT THE LITTLE TOWN of Vevey, in Switzerland, there is a particularly comfortable hotel. There are, indeed, many hotels; for the entertainment of tourists is the business of the place, which, as many travelers will remember, is seated upon the edge of a remarkably blue lake[1] – a lake that it behooves every tourist to visit. The shore of the lake presents an unbroken array of establishments of this order, of every category, from the "grand hotel" of the newest fashion, with a chalk-white front, a hundred balconies, and a dozen flags flying from its roof, to the little Swiss *pension*[2] of an elder day, with its name inscribed in German-looking lettering upon a pink or yellow wall, and an awkward summerhouse in the angle of the garden. One of the hotels at Vevey, however, is famous, even classical, being distinguished from many of

1. *lake*: Lake Geneva (French, Lac Léman).
2. *pension*: Guesthouse (French).

its upstart neighbours by an air both of luxury and of maturity. In this region, in the month of June, American travelers are extremely numerous; it may be said, indeed, that Vevey assumes at this period some of the characteristics of an American watering-place. There are sights and sounds which evoke a vision, an echo, of Newport and Saratoga.[3] There is a flitting hither and thither of "stylish" young girls, a rustling of muslin flounces, a rattle of dance-music in the morning hours, a sound of high-pitched voices at all times. You receive an impression of these things at the excellent inn of the "Trois Couronnes," and are transported in fancy to the Ocean House or to Congress Hall.[4] But at the "Trois Couronnes," it must be added, there are other features that are much at variance with these suggestions: neat German waiters, who look like secretaries of legation; Russian princesses sitting in the garden; little Polish boys walking about, held by the hand, with their governors; a view of the sunny crest of the Dent du Midi[5] and the picturesque towers of the Castle of Chillon.[6]

I hardly know whether it was the analogies or the differences that were uppermost in the mind of a young American, who, two or three years ago, sat in the garden of the "Trois Couronnes," looking about him, rather idly, at some of the graceful objects I have mentioned. It was a beautiful summer morning, and in whatever fashion the young American looked at things, they must have seemed to him charming. He had come from Geneva the day before, by the little steamer, to see his aunt, who was staying at the hotel – Geneva having been for a long time his place of residence. But his aunt had a headache – his aunt had almost always a headache – and now she was shut up in her room, smelling camphor,[7] so that he was at liberty to wander about. He was some seven-and-twenty years of age; when his friends spoke of him, they usually said that he was at Geneva, "studying." When his enemies spoke of him they said – but, after all, he had no enemies; he was an extremely amiable fellow, and universally liked. What I should say is, simply, that when certain persons spoke of him they affirmed that the reason of his spending so much time at Geneva was that he was extremely devoted to a lady who lived there – a foreign lady – a person

3. *Newport and Saratoga:* Fashionable nineteenth-century resort destinations in Rhode Island and upstate New York.
4. *Ocean House . . . Congress Hall:* Grand hotels in Newport and Saratoga Springs.
5. *Dent du Midi:* An Alpine range that rises dramatically from the Lake Geneva shore.
6. *Castle of Chillon:* Château de Chillon, a castle associated with the incarceration of the Swiss partisan, François Bonivard (1496-1570), celebrated in Byrron's 1816 poem, "The Prisoner of Chillon."
7. *camphor:* Waxlike substance with aromatic medicinal properties.

older than himself. Very few Americans – indeed I think none – had ever seen this lady, about whom there were some singular stories. But Winterbourne had an old attachment for the little metropolis of Calvinism;[8] he had been put to school there as a boy, and he had afterwards gone to college there – circumstances which had led to his forming a great many youthful friendships. Many of these he had kept, and they were a source of great satisfaction to him.

After knocking at his aunt's door and learning that she was indisposed, he had taken a walk about the town, and then he had come in to his breakfast. He had now finished his breakfast; but he was drinking a small cup of coffee, which had been served to him on a little table in the garden by one of the waiters who looked like an *attaché.*[9] At last he finished his coffee and lit a cigarette. Presently a small boy came walking along the path – an urchin of nine or ten. The child, who was diminutive for his years, had an aged expression of countenance, a pale complexion, and sharp little features. He was dressed in knickerbockers, with red stockings, which displayed his poor little spindleshanks;[10] he also wore a brilliant red cravat.[11] He carried in his hand a long alpenstock,[12] the sharp point of which he thrust into everything that he approached – the flowerbeds, the garden-benches, the trains of the ladies' dresses. In front of Winterbourne he paused, looking at him with a pair of bright, penetrating little eyes.

"Will you give me a lump of sugar?" he asked, in a sharp, hard little voice – a voice immature, and yet, somehow, not young.

Winterbourne glanced at the small table near him, on which his coffee-service rested, and saw that several morsels of sugar remained. "Yes, you may take one," he answered; "but I don't think sugar is good for little boys."

This little boy stepped forward and carefully selected three of the coveted fragments, two of which he buried in the pocket of his knickerbockers, depositing the other as promptly in another place. He poked his alpenstock, lance-fashion, into Winterbourne's bench, and tried to crack the lump of sugar with his teeth.

8. *Calvinism:* Compelled to leave his native France, John Calvin (1509-1564), a major theologian of the Protestant Reformation, sought refuge in Geneva where he established a theocracy.
9. *attaché:* A midlevel embassy staff member.
10. *spindleshanks:* Conspicuously slender and fragile-looking shins.
11. *cravat:* Necktie.
12. *alpenstock:* Long stick with a metal point, used in mountain climbing.

"Oh, blazes; it's har-r-d!"[13] he exclaimed, pronouncing the adjective in a peculiar manner.

Winterbourne had immediately perceived that he might have the honour of claiming him as a fellow-countryman. "Take care you don't hurt your teeth," he said, paternally.

"I haven't got any teeth to hurt. They have all come out. I have only got seven teeth. My mother counted them last night, and one came out right afterwards. She said she'd slap me if any more came out. I can't help it. It's this old Europe. It's the climate that makes them come out. In America they didn't come out. It's these hotels."

Winterbourne was much amused. "If you eat three lumps of sugar, your mother will certainly slap you," he said.

"She's got to give me some candy, then," rejoined his young interlocutor. "I can't get any candy here – any American candy. American candy's the best candy."

"And are American little boys the best little boys?" asked Winterbourne.

"I don't know. I'm an American boy," said the child.

"I see you are one of the best!" laughed Winterbourne.

"Are you an American man?" pursued this vivacious infant. And then, on Winterbourne's affirmative reply – "American men are the best," he declared.

His companion thanked him for the compliment; and the child, who had now got astride of his alpenstock, stood looking about him, while he attacked a second lump of sugar. Winterbourne wondered if he himself had been like this in his infancy, for he had been brought to Europe at about this age.

"Here comes my sister!" cried the child, in a moment. "She's an American girl."

Winterbourne looked along the path and saw a beautiful young lady advancing. "American girls are the best girls," he said, cheerfully, to his young companion.

"My sister ain't the best!" the child declared. "She's always blowing at me."

"I imagine that is your fault, not hers," said Winterbourne. The young lady meanwhile had drawn near. She was dressed in white muslin, with a

13. *har-r-d*: One of numerous instances in which James depicts vernacular nineteenth-century American speech. Note, also, occurrence of the phrases "I guess" and "I don't believe it!" In this era, "ain't" is a colloquial expression that does not necessarily imply lack of education.

hundred frills and flounces, and knots of pale-colored ribbon. She was bare-headed; but she balanced in her hand a large parasol, with a deep border of embroidery; and she was strikingly, admirably pretty. "How pretty they are!" thought Winterbourne, straightening himself in his seat, as if he were prepared to rise.

The young lady paused in front of his bench, near the parapet[14] of the garden, which overlooked the lake. The little boy had now converted his alpenstock into a vaulting pole, by the aid of which he was springing about in the gravel, and kicking it up not a little.

"Randolph," said the young lady, "what *are* you doing?"

"I'm going up the Alps," replied Randolph. "This is the way!" And he gave another little jump, scattering the pebbles about Winterbourne's ears.

"That's the way they come down," said Winterbourne.

"He's an American man!" cried Randolph, in his little hard voice.

The young lady gave no heed to this announcement, but looked straight at her brother. "Well, I guess you had better be quiet," she simply observed.

It seemed to Winterbourne that he had been in a manner presented. He got up and stepped slowly towards the young girl, throwing away his cigarette. "This little boy and I have made acquaintance," he said, with great civility. In Geneva, as he had been perfectly aware, a young man was not at liberty to speak to a young unmarried lady except under certain rarely-occurring conditions; but here at Vevey, what conditions could be better than these? – a pretty American girl coming and standing in front of you in a garden. This pretty American girl, however, on hearing Winterbourne's observation, simply glanced at him; she then turned her head and looked over the parapet, at the lake and the opposite mountains. He wondered whether he had gone too far; but he decided that he must advance farther, rather than retreat. While he was thinking of something else to say, the young lady turned to the little boy again.

"I should like to know where you got that pole," she said.

"I bought it!" responded Randolph.

"You don't mean to say you're going to take it to Italy."

"Yes, I am going to take it to Italy!" the child declared.

The young girl glanced over the front of her dress, and smoothed out a knot or two of ribbon. Then she rested her eyes upon the prospect again. "Well, I guess you had better leave it somewhere," she said, after a moment.

---

14. *parapet*: The walled corner of the garden that overlooks the lake.

"Are you going to Italy?" Winterbourne inquired, in a tone of great respect.

"The young lady glanced at him again. "Yes, sir," she replied. And she said nothing more.

"Are you – a – going over the Simplon?"[15] Winterbourne pursued, a little embarrassed.

"I don't know," she said. "I suppose it's some mountain. Randolph, what mountain are we going over?"

"Going where?" the child demanded.

"To Italy," Winterbourne explained.

"I don't know," said Randolph. "I don't want to go to Italy. I want to go to America."

"Oh, Italy is a beautiful place!" rejoined the young man.

"Can you get candy there?" Randolph loudly inquired.

"I hope not," said his sister. "I guess you have had enough candy, and mother thinks so too."

"I haven't had any for ever so long – for a hundred weeks!" cried the boy, still jumping about.

The young lady inspected her flounces and smoothed her ribbons again; and Winterbourne presently risked an observation upon the beauty of the view. He was ceasing to be embarrassed, for he had begun to perceive that she was not in the least embarrassed herself. There had not been the slightest alteration in her charming complexion; she was evidently neither offended nor fluttered. If she looked another way when he spoke to her, and seemed not particularly to hear him, this was simply her habit, her manner. Yet, as he talked a little more, and pointed out some of the objects of interest in the view, with which she appeared quite unacquainted, she gradually gave him more of the benefit of her glance; and then he saw that this glance was perfectly direct and unshrinking. It was not, however, what would have been called an immodest glance, for the young girl's eyes were singularly honest and fresh. They were wonderfully pretty eyes; and, indeed, Winterbourne had not seen for a long time anything prettier than his fair countrywoman's various features – her complexion, her nose, her ears, her teeth. He had a great relish for feminine beauty; he was addicted to observing and analyzing it; and as regards this young lady's face he made several observations. It was not at all insipid, but it was not exactly

15. *Simplon*: The Simplon Pass, a trans-Alpine route to Italy modernized by Napoleon's engineer between 1801 and 1804.

expressive; and though it was eminently delicate Winterbourne mentally accused it – very forgivingly – of a want of finish. He thought it very possible that Master Randolph's sister was a coquette;[16] he was sure she had a spirit of her own; but in her bright, sweet, superficial little visage there was no mockery, no irony. Before long it became obvious that she was much disposed towards conversation. She told him that they were going to Rome for the winter – she and her mother and Randolph. She asked him if he was a "real American"; she shouldn't have taken him for one; he seemed more like a German – this was said after a little hesitation, especially when he spoke. Winterbourne, laughing, answered that he had met Germans who spoke like Americans; but that he had not, so far as he remembered, met an American who spoke like a German. Then he asked her if she should not be more comfortable in sitting upon the bench which he had just quitted. She answered that she liked standing up and walking about; but she presently sat down. She told him she was from New York State – "if you know where that is." Winterbourne learned more about her by catching hold of her small, slippery brother and making him stand a few minutes by his side.

"Tell me your name, my boy," he said.

"Randolph C. Miller," said the boy, sharply. "And I'll tell you her name"; and he leveled his alpenstock at his sister.

"You had better wait till you are asked!" said this young lady, calmly.

"I should like very much to know your name," said Winterbourne.

"Her name is Daisy Miller!" cried the child. "But that isn't her real name; that isn't her name on her cards."

"It's a pity you haven't got one of my cards!" said Miss Miller.

"Her real name is Annie P. Miller," the boy went on.

"Ask him *his* name," said his sister, indicating Winterbourne.

But on this point Randolph seemed perfectly indifferent; he continued to supply information with regard to his own family. "My father's name is Ezra B. Miller," he announced. "My father ain't in Europe; my father's in a better place than Europe."

Winterbourne imagined for a moment that this was the manner in which the child had been taught to intimate that Mr. Miller had been removed to the sphere of celestial rewards. But Randolph immediately added, "My father's in Schenectady. He's got a big business. My father's rich, you bet!"

16. *coquette*: An overtly flirtatious young woman.

"Well!" ejaculated Miss Miller, lowering her parasol and looking at the embroidered border. Winterbourne presently released the child, who departed, dragging his alpenstock along the path. "He doesn't like Europe," said the young girl. "He wants to go back."

"To Schenectady, you mean?"

"Yes; he wants to go right home. He hasn't got any boys here. There is one boy here, but he always goes round with a teacher; they won't let him play."

"And your brother hasn't any teacher?" Winterbourne inquired.

"Mother thought of getting him one, to travel round with us. There was a lady told her of a very good teacher; an American lady – perhaps you know her – Mrs. Sanders. I think she came from Boston. She told her of this teacher, and we thought of getting him to travel round with us. But Randolph said he didn't want a teacher traveling round with us. He said he wouldn't have lessons when he was in the cars.[17] And we *are* in the cars about half the time. There was an English lady we met in the cars – I think her name was Miss Featherstone; perhaps you know her. She wanted to know why I didn't give Randolph lessons – give him 'instruction,' she called it. I guess he could give me more instruction than I could give him. He's very smart."

"Yes," said Winterbourne; "he seems very smart."

"Mother's going to get a teacher for him as soon as we get to Italy. Can you get good teachers in Italy?"

"Very good, I should think," said Winterbourne.

"Or else she's going to find some school. He ought to learn some more. He's only nine. He's going to college." And in this way Miss Miller continued to converse upon the affairs of her family, and upon other topics. She sat there with her extremely pretty hands, ornamented with very brilliant rings, folded in her lap, and with her pretty eyes now resting upon those of Winterbourne, now wandering over the garden, the people who passed by, and the beautiful view. She talked to Winterbourne as if she had known him a long time. He found it very pleasant. It was many years since he had heard a young girl talk so much. It might have been said of this unknown young lady, who had come and sat down beside him upon a bench, that she chattered. She was very quiet; she sat in a charming tranquil attitude, but her lips and her eyes were constantly moving. She had a soft, slender, agreeable voice, and her tone was decidedly sociable. She

17. *in the cars*: Traveling by rail.

gave Winterbourne a history of her movements and intentions, and those of her mother and brother, in Europe, and enumerated, in particular, the various hotels at which they had stopped. "That English lady, in the cars," she said – "Miss Featherstone – asked me if we didn't all live in hotels in America. I told her I had never been in so many hotels in my life as since I came to Europe. I have never seen so many – it's nothing but hotels." But Miss Miller did not make this remark with a querulous accent; she appeared to be in the best humour with everything. She declared that the hotels were very good, when once you got used to their ways, and that Europe was perfectly sweet. She was not disappointed – not a bit. Perhaps it was because she had heard so much about it before. She had ever so many intimate friends that had been there ever so many times. And then she had had ever so many dresses and things from Paris. Whenever she put on a Paris dress she felt as if she were in Europe.

"It was a kind of a wishing-cap," said Winterbourne.

"Yes," said Miss Miller, without examining this analogy; "it always made me wish I was here. But I needn't have done that for dresses. I am sure they send all the pretty ones to America; you see the most frightful things here. The only thing I don't like," she proceeded, "is the society. There isn't any society; or, if there is, I don't know where it keeps itself. Do you? I suppose there is some society somewhere, but I haven't seen anything of it. I'm very fond of society, and I have always had a great deal of it. I don't mean only in Schenectady, but in New York. I used to go to New York every winter. In New York I had lots of society. Last winter I had seventeen dinners given me; and three of them were by gentlemen," added Daisy Miller. "I have more friends in New York than in Schenectady – more gentleman friends; and more young lady friends too," she resumed in a moment. She paused again for an instant; she was looking at Winterbourne with all her prettiness in her lively eyes and in her light, slightly monotonous smile. "I have always had," she said, "a great deal of gentlemen's society."

Poor Winterbourne was amused, perplexed, and decidedly charmed. He had never yet heard a young girl express herself in just this fashion; never, at least, save in cases where to say such things seemed a kind of demonstrative evidence of a certain laxity of deportment. And yet was he to accuse Miss Daisy Miller of actual or potential *inconduite*,[18] as they said at Geneva? He felt that he had lived at Geneva so long that he had lost

18. *inconduite*: Misconduct, especially of a sexual nature (French).

a good deal; he had become dishabituated to the American tone. Never, indeed, since he had grown old enough to appreciate things, had he encountered a young American girl of so pronounced a type as this. Certainly she was very charming, but how deucedly sociable! Was she simply a pretty girl from New York State – were they all like that, the pretty girls who had a good deal of gentlemen's society? Or was she also a designing, an audacious, an unscrupulous young person? Winterbourne had lost his instinct in this matter, and his reason could not help him. Miss Daisy Miller looked extremely innocent. Some people had told him that, after all, American girls were exceedingly innocent; and others had told him that, after all, they were not. He was inclined to think Miss Daisy Miller was a flirt – a pretty American flirt. He had never, as yet, had any relations with young ladies of this category. He had known, here in Europe, two or three women – persons older than Miss Daisy Miller, and provided, for respectability's sake, with husbands – who were great coquettes – dangerous, terrible women, with whom one's relations were liable to take a serious turn. But this young girl was not a coquette in that sense; she was very unsophisticated; she was only a pretty American flirt. Winterbourne was almost grateful for having found the formula that applied to Miss Daisy Miller. He leaned back in his seat; he remarked to himself that she had the most charming nose he had ever seen; he wondered what were the regular conditions and limitations of one's intercourse with a pretty American flirt. It presently became apparent that he was on the way to learn.

"Have you been to that old castle?" asked the young girl, pointing with her parasol to the far-gleaming walls of the Château de Chillon.

"Yes, formerly, more than once," said Winterbourne. "You too, I suppose, have seen it?"

"No; we haven't been there. I want to go there dreadfully. Of course I mean to go there. I wouldn't go away from here without having seen that old castle."

"It's a very pretty excursion," said Winterbourne, "and very easy to make. You can drive, you know, or you can go by the little steamer."

"You can go in the cars," said Miss Miller.

"Yes; you can go in the cars," Winterbourne assented.

"Our courier[19] says they take you right up to the castle," the young girl continued. "We were going last week; but my mother gave out. She suffers dreadfully from dyspepsia. She said she couldn't go. Randolph wouldn't

---

19. *courier:* In this context, a personal tour guide and manager.

go either; he says he doesn't think much of old castles. But I guess we'll go this week, if we can get Randolph."

"Your brother is not interested in ancient monuments?" Winterbourne inquired, smiling.

"He says he don't care much about old castles. He's only nine. He wants to stay at the hotel. Mother's afraid to leave him alone, and the courier won't stay with him; so we haven't been to many places. But it will be too bad if we don't go up there." And Miss Miller pointed again at the Château de Chillon.

"I should think it might be arranged," said Winterbourne. "Couldn't you get some one to stay – for the afternoon – with Randolph?"

Miss Miller looked at him a moment; and then, very placidly – "I wish *you* would stay with him!" she said.

Winterbourne hesitated a moment. "I should much rather go to Chillon with you."

"With me?" asked the young girl, with the same placidity.

She didn't rise, blushing, as a young girl at Geneva would have done; and yet Winterbourne, conscious that he had been very bold, thought it possible she was offended. "With your mother," he answered very respectfully.

But it seemed that both his audacity and his respect were lost upon Miss Daisy Miller. "I guess my mother won't go, after all," she said. "She don't like to ride round in the afternoon. But did you really mean what you said just now; that you would like to go up there?"

"Most earnestly," Winterbourne declared.

"Then we may arrange it. If mother will stay with Randolph, I guess Eugenio will."

"Eugenio?" the young man inquired.

"Eugenio's our courier. He doesn't like to stay with Randolph; he's the most fastidious man I ever saw. But he's a splendid courier. I guess he'll stay at home with Randolph if mother does, and then we can go to the castle."

Winterbourne reflected for an instant as lucidly as possible – "we" could only mean Miss Daisy Miller and himself. This programme seemed almost too agreeable for credence; he felt as if he ought to kiss the young lady's hand. Possibly he would have done so – and quite spoiled the project; but at this moment another person – presumably Eugenio – appeared. A tall, handsome man, with superb whiskers, wearing a velvet morning-coat and a brilliant watch-chain, approached Miss Miller, looking sharply at her companion. "Oh, Eugenio!" said Miss Miller, with the friendliest accent.

Eugenio had looked at Winterbourne from head to foot; he now bowed gravely to the young lady. "I have the honour to inform mademoiselle that luncheon is upon the table."

Miss Miller slowly rose. "See here, Eugenio," she said. "I'm going to that old castle, any way."

"To the Château de Chillon, mademoiselle?" the courier inquired. "Mademoiselle has made arrangements?" he added, in a tone which struck Winterbourne as very impertinent.

Eugenio's tone apparently threw, even to Miss Miller's own apprehension, a slightly ironical light upon the young girl's situation. She turned to Winterbourne, blushing a little – a very little. "You won't back out?" she said.

"I shall not be happy till we go!" he protested.

"And you are staying in this hotel?" she went on. "And you are really an American?"

The courier stood looking at Winterbourne, offensively. The young man, at least, thought his manner of looking an offense to Miss Miller; it conveyed an imputation that she "picked up" acquaintances. "I shall have the honour of presenting to you a person who will tell you all about me," he said smiling, and referring to his aunt.

"Oh, well, we'll go some day," said Miss Miller. And she gave him a smile and turned away. She put up her parasol and walked back to the inn beside Eugenio. Winterbourne stood looking after her; and as she moved away, drawing her muslin furbelows over the gravel, said to himself that she had the *tournure*[20] of a princess.

He had, however, engaged to do more than proved feasible, in promising to present his aunt, Mrs. Costello, to Miss Daisy Miller. As soon as the former lady had got better of her headache he waited upon her in her apartment; and, after the proper inquiries in regard to her health, he asked her if she had observed, in the hotel, an American family – a mamma, a daughter, and a little boy.

"And a courier?" said Mrs. Costello. "Oh, yes, I have observed them. Seen them – heard them – and kept out of their way." Mrs. Costello was a widow with a fortune; a person of much distinction, who frequently intimated that, if she were not so dreadfully liable to sick-headaches, she would probably have left a deeper impress upon her time. She had a long pale face, a high nose, and a great deal of very striking white hair, which she

---

20. *tournure*: Grace but also affect (French).

wore in large puffs and *rouleaux*[21] over the top of her head. She had two sons married in New York, and another who was now in Europe. This young man was amusing himself at Hombourg,[22] and, though he was on his travels, was rarely perceived to visit any particular city at the moment selected by his mother for her own appearance there. Her nephew, who had come up to Vevey expressly to see her, was therefore more attentive than those who, as she said, were nearer to her. He had imbibed at Geneva the idea that one must always be attentive to one's aunt. Mrs. Costello had not seen him for many years, and she was greatly pleased with him, manifesting her approbation by initiating him into many of the secrets of that social sway which, as she gave him to understand, she exerted in the American capital. She admitted that she was very exclusive; but, if he were acquainted with New York, he would see that one had to be. And her picture of the minutely hierarchical constitution of the society of that city, which she presented to him in many different lights, was, to Winterbourne's imagination, almost oppressively striking.

He immediately perceived, from her tone, that Miss Daisy Miller's place in the social scale was low. "I am afraid you don't approve of them," he said.

"They are very common," Mrs. Costello declared. "They are the sort of Americans that one does one's duty by not – not accepting."

"Ah, you don't accept them?" said the young man.

"I can't, my dear Frederick. I would if I could, but I can't."

"The young girl is very pretty," said Winterbourne, in a moment.

"Of course she's pretty. But she is very common."

"I see what you mean, of course," said Winterbourne, after another pause.

"She has that charming look that they all have," his aunt resumed. "I can't think where they pick it up; and she dresses in perfection – no, you don't know how well she dresses. I can't think where they get their taste."

"But, my dear aunt, she is not, after all, a Comanche savage."[23]

"She is a young lady," said Mrs. Costello, "who has an intimacy with her mamma's courier."

---

21. *rouleaux*: Curls (French).
22. *Hombourg*: Bad Homburg, a spa in western Germany.
23. *Comanche savage*: The Comanche are a southwest Shoshone people who figured in the border wars of the 1860s and 1870s. For the class Mrs. Costello represents, Native Americans were categorically "savage" and white Americans of a presumed lower social rank were nearly so.

"An intimacy with the courier?" the young man demanded.

"Oh, the mother is just as bad! They treat the courier like a familiar friend—like a gentleman. I shouldn't wonder if he dines with them. Very likely they have never seen a man with such good manners, such fine clothes, so like a gentleman. He probably corresponds to the young lady's idea of a count. He sits with them in the garden, in the evening. I think he smokes."

Winterbourne listened with interest to these disclosures; they helped him to make up his mind about Miss Daisy. Evidently she was rather wild. "Well," he said, "I am not a courier, and yet she was very charming to me."

"You had better have said at first," said Mrs. Costello with dignity, "that you had made her acquaintance."

"We simply met in the garden, and we talked a bit."

"*Tout bonnement!*[24] And pray what did you say?"

"I said I should take the liberty of introducing her to my admirable aunt."

"I am much obliged to you."

"It was to guarantee my respectability," said Winterbourne.

"And pray who is to guarantee hers?"

"Ah, you are cruel!" said the young man. "She's a very nice young girl."

"You don't say that as if you believed it," Mrs. Costello observed.

"She is completely uncultivated," Winterbourne went on. "But she is wonderfully pretty, and, in short, she is very nice. To prove that I believe it, I am going to take her to the Château de Chillon."

"You two are going off there together? I should say it proved just the contrary. How long had you known her, may I ask, when this interesting project was formed? You haven't been twenty-four hours in the house."

"I had known her half an hour!" said Winterbourne, smiling.

"Dear me!" cried Mrs. Costello. "What a dreadful girl!"

Her nephew was silent for some moments. "You really think, then," he began, earnestly, and with a desire for trustworthy information—"you really think that——" But he paused again.

"Think what, sir?" said his aunt.

"That she is the sort of young lady who expects a man—sooner or later to carry her off?"

"I haven't the least idea what such young ladies expect a man to do. But I really think that you had better not meddle with little American

24. *tout bonnement:* Obviously (French).

girls that are uncultivated, as you call them. You have lived too long out of the country. You will be sure to make some great mistake. You are too innocent."

"My dear aunt, I am not so innocent," said Winterbourne, smiling and curling his moustache.

"You are too guilty, then!"

Winterbourne continued to curl his moustache, meditatively. "You won't let the poor girl know you then?" he asked at last.

"Is it literally true that she is going to the Château de Chillon with you?"

"I think that she fully intends it."

"Then, my dear Frederick," said Mrs. Costello, "I must decline the honour of her acquaintance. I am an old woman, but I am not too old – thank Heaven – to be shocked!"

"But don't they all do these things – the young girls in America?" Winterbourne inquired.

Mrs. Costello stared a moment. "I should like to see my granddaughters do them!" she declared, grimly.

This seemed to throw some light upon the matter, for Winterbourne remembered to have heard that his pretty cousins in New York were "tremendous flirts." If, therefore, Miss Daisy Miller exceeded the liberal margin allowed to these young ladies, it was probable that anything might be expected of her. Winterbourne was impatient to see her again, and he was vexed with himself that, by instinct, he should not appreciate her justly.

Though he was impatient to see her, he hardly knew what he should say to her about his aunt's refusal to become acquainted with her; but he discovered, promptly enough, that with Miss Daisy Miller there was no great need of walking on tiptoe. He found her that evening in the garden, wandering about in the warm starlight, like an indolent sylph, and swinging to and fro the largest fan he had ever beheld. It was ten o'clock. He had dined with his aunt, had been sitting with her since dinner, and had just taken leave of her till the morrow. Miss Daisy Miller seemed very glad to see him; she declared it was the longest evening she had ever passed.

"Have you been all alone?" he asked.

"I have been walking round with mother. But mother gets tired walking round," she answered.

"Has she gone to bed?"

"No; she doesn't like to go to bed," said the young girl. "She doesn't sleep – not three hours. She says she doesn't know how she lives. She's dreadfully nervous. I guess she sleeps more than she thinks. She's gone somewhere after Randolph; she wants to try to get him to go to bed. He doesn't like to go to bed."

"Let us hope she will persuade him," observed Winterbourne.

"She will talk to him all she can; but he doesn't like her to talk to him," said Miss Daisy, opening her fan. "She's going to try to get Eugenio to talk to him. But he isn't afraid of Eugenio. Eugenio's a splendid courier, but he can't make much impression on Randolph! I don't believe he'll go to bed before eleven." It appeared that Randolph's vigil was in fact triumphantly prolonged, for Winterbourne strolled about with the young girl for some time without meeting her mother. "I have been looking round for that lady you want to introduce me to," his companion resumed. "She's your aunt." Then, on Winterbourne's admitting the fact, and expressing some curiosity as to how she had learned it, she said she had heard all about Mrs. Costello from the chambermaid. She was very quiet and very *comme il faut*;[25] she wore white puffs; she spoke to no one, and she never dined at the *table d'hôte*.[26] Every two days she had a headache. "I think that's a lovely description, headache and all!" said Miss Daisy, chattering along in her thin, gay voice. "I want to know her ever so much. I know just what *your* aunt would be; I know I should like her. She would be very exclusive. I like a lady to be exclusive; I'm dying to be exclusive myself. Well, we *are* exclusive, mother and I. We don't speak to everyone – or they don't speak to us. I suppose it's about the same thing. Any way, I shall be ever so glad to know your aunt."

Winterbourne was embarrassed. "She would be most happy," he said; "but I am afraid those headaches will interfere."

The young girl looked at him through the dusk. "But I suppose she doesn't have a headache every day," she said, sympathetically.

Winterbourne was silent a moment. "She tells me she does," he answered at last – not knowing what to say.

Miss Daisy Miller stopped and stood looking at him. Her prettiness was still visible in the darkness; she was opening and closing her enormous fan. "She doesn't want to know me!" she said, suddenly. "Why don't you say so? You needn't be afraid. I'm not afraid!" And she gave a little laugh.

Winterbourne fancied there was a tremor in her voice; he was touched, shocked, mortified by it. "My dear young lady," he protested, "she knows no one. It's her wretched health."

25. *comme il faut*: Proper (French).
26. *table d'hôte*: Communal table at a traditional French hotel or guesthouse.

The young girl walked on a few steps, laughing still. "You needn't be afraid," she repeated. "Why should she want to know me?" Then she paused again; she was close to the parapet of the garden, and in front of her was the starlit lake. There was a vague sheen upon its surface, and in the distance were dimly-seen mountain forms. Daisy Miller looked out upon the mysterious prospect, and then she gave another little laugh. "Gracious! she *is* exclusive!" she said. Winterbourne wondered whether she was seriously wounded, and for a moment almost wished that her sense of injury might be such as to make it becoming in him to attempt to reassure and comfort her. He had a pleasant sense that she would be very approachable for consolatory purposes. He felt then, for the instant, quite ready to sacrifice his aunt, conversationally; to admit that she was a proud, rude woman, and to declare that they needn't mind her. But before he had time to commit himself to this perilous mixture of gallantry and impiety, the young lady, resuming her walk, gave an exclamation in quite another tone. "Well; here's mother! I guess she hasn't got Randolph to go to bed." The figure of a lady appeared, at a distance, very indistinct in the darkness, and advancing with a slow and wavering movement. Suddenly it seemed to pause.

"Are you sure it is your mother? Can you distinguish her in this thick dusk?" Winterbourne asked.

"Well!" cried Miss Daisy Miller, with a laugh, "I guess I know my own mother. And when she has got on my shawl, too! She is always wearing my things."

The lady in question, ceasing to advance, hovered vaguely about the spot at which she had checked her steps.

"I am afraid your mother doesn't see you," said Winterbourne. "Or perhaps," he added – thinking, with Miss Miller, the joke permissible – "perhaps she feels guilty about your shawl."

"Oh, it's a fearful old thing!" the young girl replied, serenely. "I told her she could wear it. She won't come here, because she sees you."

"Ah, then," said Winterbourne, "I had better leave you."

"Oh, no; come on!" urged Miss Daisy Miller.

"I'm afraid your mother doesn't approve of my walking with you."

Miss Miller gave him a serious glance. "It isn't for me; it's for you – that is, it's for *her*. Well; I don't know who it's for! But mother doesn't like any of my gentlemen friends. She's right down timid. She always makes a fuss if I introduce a gentleman. But I *do* introduce them – almost always. If I didn't introduce my gentlemen friends to mother," the young girl added, in her little soft, flat monotone, "I shouldn't think I was natural."

"To introduce me," said Winterbourne, "you must know my name." And he proceeded to pronounce it.

"Oh, dear; I can't say all that!" said his companion, with a laugh. But by this time they had come up to Mrs. Miller, who, as they drew near, walked to the parapet of the garden and leaned upon it, looking intently at the lake, and turning her back to them. "Mother!" said the young girl, in a tone of decision. Upon this the elder lady turned round. "Mr. Winterbourne," said Miss Daisy Miller, introducing the young man very frankly and prettily. "Common" she was, as Mrs. Costello had pronounced her; yet it was a wonder to Winterbourne that, with her commonness, she had a singularly delicate grace.

Her mother was a small, spare, light person, with a wandering eye, a very exiguous nose, and a large forehead, decorated with a certain amount of thin, much-frizzled hair. Like her daughter, Mrs. Miller was dressed with extreme elegance; she had enormous diamonds in her ears. So far as Winterbourne could observe, she gave him no greeting – she certainly was not looking at him. Daisy was near her, pulling her shawl straight. "What are you doing, poking round here?" this young lady inquired; but by no means with that harshness of accent which her choice of words may imply.

"I don't know," said her mother, turning towards the lake again.

"I shouldn't think you'd want that shawl!" Daisy exclaimed.

"Well – I do!" her mother answered, with a little laugh.

"Did you get Randolph to go to bed?" asked the young girl.

"No; I couldn't induce him," said Mrs. Miller, very gently. "He wants to talk to the waiter. He likes to talk to that waiter."

"I was telling Mr. Winterbourne," the young girl went on; and to the young man's ear her tone might have indicated that she had been uttering his name all her life.

"Oh, yes!" said Winterbourne; "I have the pleasure of knowing your son."

Randolph's mamma was silent; she turned her attention to the lake. But at last she spoke. "Well, I don't see how he lives!"

"Anyhow, it isn't so bad as it was at Dover," said Daisy Miller.

"And what occurred at Dover?" Winterbourne asked.

"He wouldn't go to bed at all. I guess he sat up all night – in the public parlour. He wasn't in bed at twelve o'clock: I know that."

"It was half-past twelve," declared Mrs. Miller, with mild emphasis.

"Does he sleep much during the day?" Winterbourne demanded.

"I guess he doesn't sleep much," Daisy rejoined.

"I wish he would!" said her mother. "It seems as if he couldn't."

"I think he's real tiresome," Daisy pursued.

Then, for some moments, there was silence. "Well, Daisy Miller," said the elder lady, presently, "I shouldn't think you'd want to talk against your own brother!"

"Well, he *is* tiresome, mother," said Daisy, quite without the asperity of a retort.

"He's only nine," urged Mrs. Miller.

"Well, he wouldn't go to that castle," said the young girl. "I'm going there with Mr. Winterbourne."

To this announcement, very placidly made, Daisy's mamma offered no response. Winterbourne took for granted that she deeply disapproved of the projected excursion; but he said to himself that she was a simple, easily-managed person, and that a few deferential protestations would take the edge from her displeasure. "Yes," he began; "your daughter has kindly allowed me the honour of being her guide."

Mrs. Miller's wandering eyes attached themselves, with a sort of appealing air, to Daisy, who, however, strolled a few steps farther, gently humming to herself. "I presume you will go in the cars," said her mother.

"Yes; or in the boat," said Winterbourne.

"Well, of course, I don't know," Mrs. Miller rejoined. "I have never been to that castle."

"It is a pity you shouldn't go," said Winterbourne, beginning to feel reassured as to her opposition. And yet he was quite prepared to find that, as a matter of course, she meant to accompany her daughter.

"We've been thinking ever so much about going," she pursued; "but it seems as if we couldn't. Of course Daisy – she wants to go round. But there's a lady here – I don't know her name – she says she shouldn't think we'd want to go to see castles *here*; she should think we'd want to wait till we got to Italy. It seems as if there would be so many there," continued Mrs. Miller, with an air of increasing confidence. "Of course, we only want to see the principal ones. We visited several in England," she presently added.

"Ah, yes! in England there are beautiful castles," said Winterbourne. "But Chillon, here, is very well worth seeing."

"Well, if Daisy feels up to it ——," said Mrs. Miller, in a tone impregnated with a sense of the magnitude of the enterprise. "It seems as if there was nothing she wouldn't undertake."

"Oh, I think she'll enjoy it!" Winterbourne declared. And he desired more and more to make it a certainty that he was to have the privilege of a *tête-à-tête*[27] with the young lady, who was still strolling along in front of them, softly vocalising. "You are not disposed, madam," he inquired, "to undertake it yourself?"

Daisy's mother looked at him, an instant, askance, and then walked forward in silence. Then – "I guess she had better go alone," she said, simply. Winterbourne observed to himself that this was a very different type of maternity from that of the vigilant matrons who massed themselves in the forefront of social intercourse in the dark old city at the other end of the lake. But his meditations were interrupted by hearing his name very distinctly pronounced by Mrs. Miller's unprotected daughter.

"Mr. Winterbourne!" murmured Daisy.

"Mademoiselle!" said the young man.

"Don't you want to take me out in a boat?"

"At present?" he asked.

"Of course!" said Daisy.

"Well, Annie Miller!" exclaimed her mother.

"I beg you, madam, to let her go," said Winterbourne, ardently; for he had never yet enjoyed the sensation of guiding through the summer starlight a skiff freighted with a fresh and beautiful young girl.

"I shouldn't think she'd want to," said her mother. "I should think she'd rather go indoors."

"I'm sure Mr. Winterbourne wants to take me," Daisy declared. "He's so awfully devoted!"

"I will row you over to Chillon, in the starlight."

"I don't believe it!" said Daisy.

"Well!" ejaculated the elder lady again.

"You haven't spoken to me for half an hour," her daughter went on.

"I have been having some very pleasant conversation with your mother," said Winterbourne.

"Well; I want you to take me out in a boat!" Daisy repeated. They had all stopped, and she had turned round and was looking at Winterbourne. Her face wore a charming smile, her pretty eyes were gleaming, she was swinging her great fan about. No; it's impossible to be prettier than that, thought Winterbourne.

"There are half a dozen boats moored at that landing-place," he said, pointing to certain steps which descended from the garden to the lake. "If you will do me the honour to accept my arm, we will go and select one of them."

---

27. *tête-à-tête*: Private conversation (French).

Daisy stood there smiling; she threw back her head and gave a little, light laugh. "I like a gentleman to be formal!" she declared.

"I assure you it's a formal offer."

"I was bound I would make you say something," Daisy went on.

"You see it's not very difficult," said Winterbourne. "But I am afraid you are chaffing me."

"I think not, sir," remarked Mrs. Miller, very gently.

"Do, then, let me give you a row," he said to the young girl.

"It's quite lovely, the way you say that!" cried Daisy.

"It will be still more lovely to do it."

"Yes, it would be lovely!" said Daisy. But she made no movement to accompany him; she only stood there laughing.

"I should think you had better find out what time it is," interposed her mother.

"It is eleven o'clock, madam," said a voice, with a foreign accent, out of the neighbouring darkness; and Winterbourne, turning, perceived the florid personage who was in attendance upon the two ladies. He had apparently just approached.

"Oh, Eugenio," said Daisy, "I am going out in a boat!"

Eugenio bowed. "At eleven o'clock, mademoiselle?"

"I am going with Mr. Winterbourne. This very minute."

"Do tell her she can't," said Mrs. Miller to the courier.

"I think you had better not go out in a boat, mademoiselle," Eugenio declared.

Winterbourne wished to Heaven this pretty girl were not so familiar with her courier; but he said nothing.

"I suppose you don't think it's proper!" Daisy exclaimed. "Eugenio doesn't think anything's proper."

"I am at your service," said Winterbourne.

"Does mademoiselle propose to go alone?" asked Eugenio of Mrs. Miller.

"Oh, no; with this gentleman!" answered Daisy's mamma.

The courier looked for a moment at Winterbourne – the latter thought he was smiling – and then, solemnly, with a bow, "As mademoiselle pleases!" he said.

"Oh, I hoped you would make a fuss!" said Daisy. "I don't care to go now."

"I myself shall make a fuss if you don't go," said Winterbourne.

"That's all I want – a little fuss!" And the young girl began to laugh again.

"Mr. Randolph has gone to bed!" the courier announced, frigidly.

"Oh, Daisy; now we can go!" said Mrs. Miller.

Daisy turned away from Winterbourne, looking at him, smiling, and fanning herself. "Good night," she said; "I hope you are disappointed, or disgusted, or something!"

He looked at her, taking the hand she offered him. "I am puzzled," he answered.

"Well; I hope it won't keep you awake!" she said, very smartly; and, under the escort of the privileged Eugenio, the two ladies passed towards the house.

Winterbourne stood looking after them; he was indeed puzzled. He lingered beside the lake for a quarter of an hour, turning over the mystery of the young girl's sudden familiarities and caprices. But the only very definite conclusion he came to was that he should enjoy deucedly "going off" with her somewhere.

Two days afterwards he went off with her to the Castle of Chillon. He waited for her in the large hall of the hotel, where the couriers, the servants, the foreign tourists were lounging about and staring. It was not the place he should have chosen, but she had appointed it. She came tripping downstairs, buttoning her long gloves, squeezing her folded parasol against her pretty figure, dressed in the perfection of a soberly elegant travelling-costume. Winterbourne was a man of imagination and, as our ancestors used to say, sensibility; as he looked at her dress and, on the great staircase, her little rapid, confiding step, he felt as if there were something romantic going forward. He could have believed he was going to elope with her. He passed out with her among all the idle people that were assembled there; they were all looking at her very hard; she had begun to chatter as soon as she joined him. Winterbourne's preference had been that they should be conveyed to Chillon in a carriage; but she expressed a lively wish to go in the little steamer; she declared that she had a passion for steamboats. There was always such a lovely breeze upon the water, and you saw such lots of people. The sail was not long, but Winterbourne's companion found time to say a great many things. To the young man himself their little excursion was so much of an escapade – an adventure – that, even allowing for her habitual sense of freedom, he had some expectation of seeing her regard it in the same way. But it must be confessed that, in this particular, he was disappointed. Daisy Miller was extremely animated, she was in charming spirits; but she was apparently not at all excited; she was not fluttered; she avoided neither his eyes nor those of any one else; she blushed neither when she looked at him nor when she felt that people were looking at her. People continued to look at her a great deal, and Winterbourne took much satisfaction in his pretty companion's distinguished air. He had been a little afraid that she would talk loud, laugh overmuch, and even, perhaps, desire to move about the boat a good deal. But he quite forgot his fears; he sat smiling, with his eyes upon her face, while, without moving from her place, she delivered herself of a great number of original reflections. It was the most charming garrulity he had ever heard. He had assented to the idea that she was "common"; but was she so, after all, or was he simply getting used to her commonness? Her conversation was chiefly of what metaphysicians term the objective cast; but every now and then it took a subjective turn.

"What on *earth* are you so grave about?" she suddenly demanded, fixing her agreeable eyes upon Winterbourne's.

"Am I grave?" he asked. "I had an idea I was grinning from ear to ear."

"You look as if you were taking me to a funeral. If that's a grin, your ears are very near together."

"Should you like me to dance a hornpipe on the deck?"

"Pray do, and I'll carry round your hat. It will pay the expenses of our journey."

"I never was better pleased in my life," murmured Winterbourne.

She looked at him a moment, and then burst into a little laugh. "I like to make you say those things! You're a queer mixture!"

In the castle, after they had landed, the subjective element decidedly prevailed. Daisy tripped about the vaulted chambers, rustled her skirts in the corkscrew staircases, flirted back with a pretty little cry and a shudder from the edge of the *oubliettes*,[28] and turned a singularly well-shaped ear to everything that Winterbourne told her about the place. But he saw that she cared very little for feudal antiquities, and that the dusky traditions of Chillon made but a slight impression upon her. They had the good fortune to have been able to walk about without other companionship than that of the custodian; and Winterbourne arranged with this functionary that they should not be hurried – that they should linger and pause wherever they chose. The custodian interpreted the bargain generously – Winterbourne, on his side, had been generous – and ended by leaving them quite to themselves. Miss Miller's observations were not remarkable for logical consistency; for anything she wanted to say she was sure to find a pretext. She found a great many pretexts in the rugged embrasures of Chillon for asking

28. *oubliettes*: Dungeons (French).

Winterbourne sudden questions about himself – his family, his previous history, his tastes, his habits, his intentions – and for supplying information upon corresponding points in her own personality. Of her own tastes, habits, and intentions Miss Miller was prepared to give the most definite, and indeed the most favorable, account.

"Well; I hope you know enough!" she said to her companion, after he had told her the history of the unhappy Bonivard.[29] "I never saw a man that knew so much!" The history of Bonivard had evidently, as they say, gone into one ear and out of the other. But Daisy went on to say that she wished Winterbourne would travel with them and "go round" with them; they might know something, in that case. "Don't you want to come and teach Randolph?" she asked. Winterbourne said that nothing could possibly please him so much; but that he had unfortunately other occupations. "Other occupations? I don't believe it!" said Miss Daisy. "What do you mean? You are not in business." The young man admitted that he was not in business; but he had engagements which, even within a day or two, would force him to go back to Geneva. "Oh, bother!" she said: "I don't believe it!" and she began to talk about something else. But a few moments later, when he was pointing out to her the pretty design of an antique fireplace, she broke out irrelevantly, "You don't mean to say you are going back to Geneva?"

"It is a melancholy fact that I shall have to return to Geneva tomorrow."

"Well, Mr. Winterbourne," said Daisy; "I think you're horrid!"

"Oh, don't say such dreadful things!" said Winterbourne – "just at the last!"

"The last!" cried the young girl; "I call it the first. I have half a mind to leave you here and go straight back to the hotel alone." And for the next ten minutes she did nothing but call him horrid. Poor Winterbourne was fairly bewildered; no young lady had as yet done him the honour to be so agitated by the announcement of his movements. His companion, after this, ceased to pay any attention to the curiosities of Chillon or the beauties of the lake; she opened fire upon the mysterious charmer in Geneva whom she appeared to have instantly taken it for granted that he was hurrying back to see. How did Miss Daisy Miller know that there was a charmer in Geneva? Winterbourne, who denied the existence of such a

---

29. *Bonivard*: François Bonivard (1496-1570). See note 6. Bonivard was imprisoned for seven years in Chillon Castle.

person, was quite unable to discover; and he was divided between amazement at the rapidity of her induction and amusement at the frankness of her *persiflage*.[30] She seemed to him, in all this, an extraordinary mixture of innocence and crudity. "Does she never allow you more than three days at a time?" asked Daisy, ironically. "Doesn't she give you a vacation in summer? There's no one so hard worked but they can get leave to go off somewhere at this season. I suppose, if you stay another day, she'll come after you in the boat. Do wait over till Friday, and I will go down to the landing to see her arrive!" Winterbourne began to think he had been wrong to feel disappointed in the temper in which the young lady had embarked. If he had missed the personal accent, the personal accent was now making its appearance. It sounded very distinctly, at last, in her telling him she would stop "teasing" him if he would promise her solemnly to come down to Rome in the winter.

"That's not a difficult promise to make," said Winterbourne. "My aunt has taken an apartment in Rome for the winter, and has already asked me to come and see her."

"I don't want you to come for your aunt," said Daisy; "I want you to come for me." And this was the only allusion that the young man was ever to hear her make to his invidious kinswoman. He declared that, at any rate, he would certainly come. After this Daisy stopped teasing. Winterbourne took a carriage, and they drove back to Vevey in the dusk; the young girl was very quiet.

In the evening Winterbourne mentioned to Mrs. Costello that he had spent the afternoon at Chillon, with Miss Daisy Miller.

"The Americans – of the courier?" asked this lady.

"Ah, happily," said Winterbourne, "the courier stayed at home."

"She went with you all alone?"

"All alone."

Mrs. Costello sniffed a little at her smelling-bottle. "And that," she exclaimed, "is the young person whom you wanted me to know!"

---

30. *persiflage*: Banter (French).

Part II.

WINTERBOURNE, WHO HAD returned to Geneva the day after his excursion to Chillon, went to Rome towards the end of January. His aunt had been established there for several weeks, and he had received a couple of letters from her. "Those people you were so devoted to last summer at Vevey have turned up here, courier and all," she wrote. "They seem to have made several acquaintances, but the courier continues to be the most *intime*.[31] The young lady, however, is also very intimate with some third-rate Italians, with whom she rackets about in a way that makes much talk. Bring me that pretty novel of Cherbuliez's – 'Paule Méré'[32] – and don't come later than the 23rd."

In the natural course of events, Winterbourne, on arriving in Rome, would presently have ascertained Mrs. Miller's address at the American banker's, and have gone to pay his compliments to Miss Daisy. "After what happened at Vevey I think I may certainly call upon them," he said to Mrs. Costello.

"If, after what happens – at Vevey and everywhere – you desire to keep up the acquaintance, you are very welcome. Of course a man may know everyone. Men are welcome to the privilege!"

"Pray what is it that happens – here, for instance?" Winterbourne demanded.

"The girl goes about alone with her foreigners. As to what happens further, you must apply elsewhere for information. She has picked up half-a-dozen of the regular Roman fortune-hunters, and she takes them about to people's houses. When she comes to a party she brings with her a gentleman with a good deal of manner and a wonderful moustache."

"And where is the mother?"

"I haven't the least idea. They are very dreadful people."

Winterbourne meditated a moment. "They are very ignorant – very innocent only. Depend upon it they are not bad."

"They are hopelessly vulgar," said Mrs. Costello. "Whether or not being hopelessly vulgar is being 'bad' is a question for the metaphysicians. They are bad enough to dislike, at any rate; and for this short life that is quite enough."

---

31. *intime*: Intimate (French), here with the connotation of "familiar."
32. *Paule Méré*: A novel by Charles Cherbuliez (1829–1899) that features a heroine who, like Daisy, violates social codes and becomes the victim of unrelenting gossip.

The news that Daisy Miller was surrounded by half-a-dozen wonderful moustaches checked Winterbourne's impulse to go straightway to see her. He had perhaps not definitely flattered himself that he had made an ineffaceable impression upon her heart, but he was annoyed at hearing of a state of affairs so little in harmony with an image that had lately flitted in and out of his own meditations; the image of a very pretty girl looking out of an old Roman window and asking herself urgently when Mr. Winterbourne would arrive. If, however, he determined to wait a little before reminding Miss Miller of his claims to her consideration, he went very soon to call upon two or three other friends. One of these friends was an American lady who had spent several winters at Geneva, where she had placed her children at school. She was a very accomplished woman, and she lived in the Via Gregoriana. Winterbourne found her in a little crimson drawing-room, on a third floor; the room was filled with southern sunshine. He had not been there ten minutes when the servant came in, announcing "Madame Mila!" This announcement was presently followed by the entrance of little Randolph Miller, who stopped in the middle of the room and stood staring at Winterbourne. An instant later his pretty sister crossed the threshold; and then, after a considerable interval, Mrs. Miller slowly advanced.

"I know you!" said Randolph.

"I'm sure you know a great many things," exclaimed Winterbourne, taking him by the hand. "How is your education coming on?"

Daisy was exchanging greetings very prettily with her hostess; but when she heard Winterbourne's voice she quickly turned her head. "Well, I declare!" she said.

"I told you I should come, you know," Winterbourne rejoined, smiling.

"Well – I didn't believe it," said Miss Daisy.

"I am much obliged to you," laughed the young man.

"You might have come to see me!" said Daisy.

"I arrived only yesterday."

"I don't believe that!" the young girl declared.

Winterbourne turned with a protesting smile to her mother; but this lady evaded his glance, and, seating herself, fixed her eyes upon her son. "We've got a bigger place than this," said Randolph. "It's all gold on the walls."

Mrs. Miller turned uneasily in her chair. "I told you if I were to bring you, you would say something!" she murmured.

"I told *you!*" Randolph exclaimed. "I tell *you,* sir!" he added jocosely, giving Winterbourne a thump on the knee. "It *is* bigger, too!"

Daisy had entered upon a lively conversation with her hostess; Winterbourne judged it becoming to address a few words to her mother. "I hope you have been well since we parted at Vevey," he said.

Mrs. Miller now certainly looked at him – at his chin. "Not very well, sir," she answered.

"She's got the dyspepsia,"[33] said Randolph. "I've got it too. Father's got it. I've got it most!"

This announcement, instead of embarrassing Mrs. Miller, seemed to relieve her. "I suffer from the liver," she said. "I think it's this climate; it's less bracing than Schenectady, especially in the winter season. I don't know whether you know we reside at Schenectady. I was saying to Daisy that I certainly hadn't found anyone like Dr. Davis, and I didn't believe I should. Oh, at Schenectady, he stands first; they think everything of him. He has so much to do, and yet there was nothing he wouldn't do for me. He said he never saw anything like my dyspepsia, but he was bound to cure it. I'm sure there was nothing he wouldn't try. He was just going to try something new when we came off. Mr. Miller wanted Daisy to see Europe for herself. But I wrote to Mr. Miller that it seems as if I couldn't get on without Dr. Davis. At Schenectady he stands at the very top; and there's a great deal of sickness there, too. It affects my sleep."

Winterbourne had a good deal of pathological gossip with Dr. Davis's patient, during which Daisy chattered unremittingly to her own companion. The young man asked Mrs. Miller how she was pleased with Rome. "Well, I must say I am disappointed," she answered. "We had heard so much about it; I suppose we had heard too much. But we couldn't help that. We had been led to expect something different."

"Ah, wait a little, and you will become very fond of it," said Winterbourne.

"I hate it worse and worse every day!" cried Randolph.

"You are like the infant Hannibal,"[34] said Winterbourne.

"No, I ain't!" Randolph declared, at a venture.

"You are not much like an infant," said his mother. "But we have seen places," she resumed, "that I should put a long way before Rome." And in reply to Winterbourne's interrogation, "There's Zurich," she concluded; "I think Zurich is lovely; and we hadn't heard half so much about it."

33. *dyspepsia*: Chronic indigestion.
34. *Hannibal*: Carthaginian military commander (247-182 B.C.E.) whose army's invasion of the Italian Peninsula during the Second Punic War was accomplished by crossing the Alps on elephants.

"The best place we've seen is the City of Richmond!" said Randolph.

"He means the ship," his mother explained. "We crossed in that ship. Randolph had a good time on the City of Richmond."

"It's the best place I've seen," the child repeated. "Only it was turned the wrong way."

"Well, we've got to turn the right way some time," said Mrs. Miller, with a little laugh. Winterbourne expressed the hope that her daughter at least found some gratification in Rome, and she declared that Daisy was quite carried away. "It's on account of the society – the society's splendid. She goes round everywhere; she has made a great number of acquaintances. Of course she goes round more than I do. I must say they have been very sociable; they have taken her right in. And then she knows a great many gentlemen. Oh, she thinks there's nothing like Rome. Of course, it's a great deal pleasanter for a young lady if she knows plenty of gentlemen."

By this time Daisy had turned her attention again to Winterbourne. "I've been telling Mrs. Walker how mean you were!" the young girl announced.

"And what is the evidence you have offered?" asked Winterbourne, rather annoyed at Miss Miller's want of appreciation of the zeal of an admirer who on his way down to Rome had stopped neither at Bologna nor at Florence, simply because of a certain sentimental impatience. He remembered that a cynical compatriot had once told him that American women – the pretty ones, and this gave a largeness to the axiom – were at once the most exacting in the world and the least endowed with a sense of indebtedness.

"Why, you were awfully mean at Vevey," said Daisy. "You wouldn't do anything. You wouldn't stay there when I asked you."

"My dearest young lady," cried Winterbourne, with eloquence, "have I come all the way to Rome to encounter your reproaches?"

"Just hear him say that!" said Daisy to her hostess, giving a twist to a bow on this lady's dress. "Did you ever hear anything so quaint?"

"So quaint, my dear?" murmured Mrs. Walker, in the tone of a partisan of Winterbourne.

"Well, I don't know," said Daisy, fingering Mrs. Walker's ribbons. "Mrs. Walker, I want to tell you something."

"Motherr," interposed Randolph, with his rough ends to his words, "I tell you you've got to go. Eugenio'll raise something!"

"I'm not afraid of Eugenio," said Daisy, with a toss of her head. "Look here, Mrs. Walker," she went on, "you know I'm coming to your party."

"I am delighted to hear it."

"I've got a lovely dress!"

"I am very sure of that."

"But I want to ask a favour – permission to bring a friend."

"I shall be happy to see any of your friends," said Mrs. Walker, turning with a smile to Mrs. Miller.

"Oh, they are not my friends," answered Daisy's mamma, smiling shyly, in her own fashion. "I never spoke to them!"

"It's an intimate friend of mine – Mr. Giovanelli," said Daisy, without a tremor in her clear little voice or a shadow on her brilliant little face.

Mrs. Walker was silent a moment, she gave a rapid glance at Winterbourne. "I shall be glad to see Mr. Giovanelli," she then said.

"He's an Italian," Daisy pursued, with the prettiest serenity. "He's a great friend of mine – he's the handsomest man in the world – except Mr. Winterbourne! He knows plenty of Italians, but he wants to know some Americans. He thinks ever so much of Americans. He's tremendously clever. He's perfectly lovely!"

It was settled that this brilliant personage should be brought to Mrs. Walker's party, and then Mrs. Miller prepared to take her leave. "I guess we'll go back to the hotel," she said.

"You may go back to the hotel, mother, but I'm going to take a walk," said Daisy.

"She's going to walk with Mr. Giovanelli," Randolph proclaimed.

"I am going to the Pincio,"[35] said Daisy, smiling.

"Alone, my dear – at this hour?" Mrs. Walker asked. The afternoon was drawing to a close – it was the hour for the throng of carriages and of contemplative pedestrians. "I don't think it's safe, my dear," said Mrs. Walker.

"Neither do I," subjoined Mrs. Miller. "You'll get the fever[36] as sure as you live. Remember what Dr. Davis told you!"

"Give her some medicine before she goes," said Randolph.

The company had risen to its feet; Daisy, still showing her pretty teeth, bent over and kissed her hostess. "Mrs. Walker, you are too perfect," she said. "I'm not going alone; I am going to meet a friend."

35. *Pincio*: Pincian Hill and Gardens in northeast Rome, which commands panoramic views of the city.
36. *fever*: Roman fever, a potent strain of malaria. Romans understood the association of the fever with nighttime excursions before medical research linked the disease to the nocturnal activity of mosquitoes.

"Your friend won't keep you from getting the fever," Mrs. Miller observed.

"Is it Mr. Giovanelli?" asked the hostess.

Winterbourne was watching the young girl; at this question his attention quickened. She stood there smiling and smoothing her bonnet ribbons; she glanced at Winterbourne. Then, while she glanced and smiled, she answered without a shade of hesitation, "Mr. Giovanelli – the beautiful Giovanelli."

"My dear young friend," said Mrs. Walker, taking her hand, pleadingly, "don't walk off to the Pincio at this hour to meet a beautiful Italian."

"Well, he speaks English," said Mrs. Miller.

"Gracious me!" Daisy exclaimed, "I don't want to do anything improper. There's an easy way to settle it." She continued to glance at Winterbourne. "The Pincio is only a hundred yards distant, and if Mr. Winterbourne were as polite as he pretends he would offer to walk with me!"

Winterbourne's politeness hastened to affirm itself, and the young girl gave him gracious leave to accompany her. They passed downstairs before her mother, and at the door Winterbourne perceived Mrs. Miller's carriage drawn up, with the ornamental courier whose acquaintance he had made at Vevey seated within. "Good-by, Eugenio!" cried Daisy, "I'm going to take a walk." The distance from the Via Gregoriana to the beautiful garden at the other end of the Pincian Hill is, in fact, rapidly traversed. As the day was splendid, however, and the concourse of vehicles, walkers, and loungers numerous, the young Americans found their progress much delayed. This fact was highly agreeable to Winterbourne, in spite of his consciousness of his singular situation. The slow-moving, idly-gazing Roman crowd bestowed much attention upon the extremely pretty young foreign lady who was passing through it upon his arm; and he wondered what on earth had been in Daisy's mind when she proposed to expose herself, unattended, to its appreciation. His own mission, to her sense, apparently, was to consign her to the hands of Mr. Giovanelli; but Winterbourne, at once annoyed and gratified, resolved that he would do no such thing.

"Why haven't you been to see me?" asked Daisy. "You can't get out of that."

"I have had the honour of telling you that I have only just stepped out of the train."

"You must have stayed in the train a good while after it stopped!" cried the young girl, with her little laugh. "I suppose you were asleep. You have had time to go to see Mrs. Walker."

"I knew Mrs. Walker – " Winterbourne began to explain.

"I knew where you knew her. You knew her at Geneva. She told me so. Well, you knew me at Vevey. That's just as good. So you ought to have come." She asked him no other question than this; she began to prattle about her own affairs. "We've got splendid rooms at the hotel; Eugenio says they're the best rooms in Rome. We are going to stay all winter – if we don't die of the fever; and I guess we'll stay then. It's a great deal nicer than I thought; I thought it would be fearfully quiet; I was sure it would be awfully poky. I was sure we should be going round all the time with one of those dreadful old men that explain about the pictures and things. But we only had about a week of that, and now I'm enjoying myself. I know ever so many people, and they are all so charming. The society's extremely select. There are all kinds – English, and Germans, and Italians. I think I like the English best. I like their style of conversation. But there are some lovely Americans. I never saw anything so hospitable. There's something or other every day. There's not much dancing; but I must say I never thought dancing was everything. I was always fond of conversation. I guess I shall have plenty at Mrs. Walker's – her rooms are so small." When they had passed the gate of the Pincian Gardens, Miss Miller began to wonder where Mr. Giovanelli might be. "We had better go straight to that place in front," she said, "where you look at the view."

"I certainly shall not help you to find him," Winterbourne declared.

"Then I shall find him without you," said Miss Daisy.

"You certainly won't leave me!" cried Winterbourne.

She burst into her little laugh. "Are you afraid you'll get lost – or run over? But there's Giovanelli, leaning against that tree. He's staring at the women in the carriages: did you ever see anything so cool?"

Winterbourne perceived at some distance a little man standing with folded arms, nursing his cane. He had a handsome face, an artfully poised hat, a glass in one eye and a nosegay in his button-hole. Winterbourne looked at him a moment and then said, "Do you mean to speak to that man?"

"Do I mean to speak to him? Why, you don't suppose I mean to communicate by signs?"

"Pray understand, then," said Winterbourne, "that I intend to remain with you."

Daisy stopped and looked at him, without a sign of troubled consciousness in her face; with nothing but the presence of her charming eyes and her happy dimples. "Well, she's a cool one!" thought the young man.

"I don't like the way you say that," said Daisy. "It's too imperious."

"I beg your pardon if I say it wrong. The main point is to give you an idea of my meaning."

The young girl looked at him more gravely, but with eyes that were prettier than ever. "I have never allowed a gentleman to dictate to me, or to interfere with anything I do."

"I think you have made a mistake," said Winterbourne. "You should sometimes listen to a gentleman – the right one."

Daisy began to laugh again. "I do nothing but listen to gentlemen!" she exclaimed. "Tell me if Mr. Giovanelli is the right one?"

The gentleman with the nosegay in his bosom had now perceived our two friends, and was approaching the young girl with obsequious rapidity. He bowed to Winterbourne as well as to the latter's companion; he had a brilliant smile, an intelligent eye; Winterbourne thought him not a bad-looking fellow. But he nevertheless said to Daisy – "No, he's not the right one."

Daisy evidently had a natural talent for performing introductions; she mentioned the name of each of her companions to the other. She strolled along with one of them on each side of her; Mr. Giovanelli, who spoke English very cleverly – Winterbourne afterwards learned that he had practised the idiom upon a great many American heiresses – addressed her a great deal of very polite nonsense; he was extremely urbane, and the young American, who said nothing, reflected upon that profundity of Italian cleverness which enables people to appear more gracious in proportion as they are more acutely disappointed. Giovanelli, of course, had counted upon something more intimate; he had not bargained for a party of three. But he kept his temper in a manner which suggested far-stretching intentions. Winterbourne flattered himself that he had taken his measure. "He is not a gentleman," said the young American; "he is only a clever imitation of one. He is a music-master, or a penny-a-liner, or a third-rate artist. Damn his good looks!" Mr. Giovanelli had certainly a very pretty face; but Winterbourne felt a superior indignation at his own lovely fellow-countrywoman's not knowing the difference between a spurious gentleman and a real one. Giovanelli chattered and jested and made himself wonderfully agreeable. It was true that if he was an imitation the imitation was brilliant. "Nevertheless," Winterbourne said to himself, "a nice girl ought to know!" And then he came back to the question whether this was in fact a nice girl. Would a nice girl – even allowing for her being a little American flirt – make a rendezvous with a presumably low-lived foreigner? The rendezvous in this case, indeed, had been in broad day-light, and in the most crowded corner of Rome; but was it not impossible to regard the choice of these circumstances as a proof of extreme cynicism? Singular though it may seem, Winterbourne was vexed that the young girl, in joining her *amoroso*,[37] should not appear more impatient of his own company, and he was vexed because of his inclination. It was impossible to regard her as a perfectly well-conducted young lady; she was wanting in a certain indispensable delicacy. It would therefore simplify matters greatly to be able to treat her as the object of one of those sentiments which are called by romancers "lawless passions." That she should seem to wish to get rid of him would help him to think more lightly of her, and to be able to think more lightly of her would make her much less perplexing. But Daisy, on this occasion, continued to present herself as an inscrutable combination of audacity and innocence.

She had been walking some quarter of an hour, attended by her two cavaliers, and responding in a tone of very childish gaiety, as it seemed to Winterbourne, to the pretty speeches of Mr. Giovanelli, when a carriage that had detached itself from the revolving train drew up beside the path. At the same moment Winterbourne perceived that his friend Mrs. Walker – the lady whose house he had lately left – was seated in the vehicle and was beckoning to him. Leaving Miss Miller's side, he hastened to obey her summons. Mrs. Walker was flushed; she wore an excited air. "It is really too dreadful," she said. "That girl must not do this sort of thing. She must not walk here with you two men. Fifty people have noticed her."

Winterbourne raised his eyebrows. "I think it's a pity to make too much fuss about it."

"It's a pity to let the girl ruin herself!"

"She is very innocent," said Winterbourne.

"She's very crazy!" cried Mrs. Walker. "Did you ever see anything so imbecile as her mother? After you had all left me, just now, I could not sit still for thinking of it. It seemed too pitiful, not even to attempt to save her. I ordered the carriage and put on my bonnet, and came here as quickly as possible. Thank heaven, I have found you!"

"What do you propose to do with us?" asked Winterbourne, smiling.

"To ask her to get in, to drive her about here for half-an-hour, so that the world may see she is not running absolutely wild, and then to take her safely home."

"I don't think it's a very happy thought," said Winterbourne; "but you can try."

37. *amoroso*: Lover (Italian).

Mrs. Walker tried. The young man went in pursuit of Miss Miller, who had simply nodded and smiled at his interlocutor in the carriage, and had gone her way with her companion. Daisy, on learning that Mrs. Walker wished to speak to her, retraced her steps with a perfect good grace and with Mr. Giovanelli at her side. She declared that she was delighted to have a chance to present this gentleman to Mrs. Walker. She immediately achieved the introduction, and declared that she had never in her life seen anything so lovely as Mrs. Walker's carriage-rug.

"I am glad you admire it," said this lady, smiling sweetly. "Will you get in and let me put it over you?"

"Oh, no, thank you," said Daisy. "I shall admire it much more as I see you driving round with it."

"Do get in and drive with me," said Mrs. Walker.

"That would be charming, but it's so enchanting just as I am!" and Daisy gave a brilliant glance at the gentlemen on either side of her.

"It may be enchanting, dear child, but it is not the custom here," urged Mrs. Walker, leaning forward in her victoria[38] with her hands devoutly clasped.

"Well, it ought to be, then!" said Daisy. "If I didn't walk I should expire."

"You should walk with your mother, dear," cried the lady from Geneva, losing patience.

"With my mother dear!" exclaimed the young girl. Winterbourne saw that she scented interference. "My mother never walked ten steps in her life. And then, you know," she added with a laugh, "I am more than five years old."

"You are old enough to be more reasonable. You are old enough, dear Miss Miller, to be talked about."

Daisy looked at Mrs. Walker, smiling intensely. "Talked about? What do you mean?"

"Come into my carriage and I will tell you."

Daisy turned her quickened glance again from one of the gentlemen beside her to the other. Mr. Giovanelli was bowing to and fro, rubbing down his gloves and laughing very agreeably; Winterbourne thought it a most unpleasant scene. "I don't think I want to know what you mean," said Daisy presently. "I don't think I should like it."

Winterbourne wished that Mrs. Walker would tuck in her carriage-rug and drive away; but this lady did not enjoy being defied, as she afterwards

---

38. *victoria*: A four-wheeled, two-seat carriage of French origin favored by fashionable women of the era.

told him. "Should you prefer being thought a very reckless girl?" she demanded.

"Gracious!" exclaimed Daisy. She looked again at Mr. Giovanelli, then she turned to Winterbourne. There was a little pink flush in her cheek; she was tremendously pretty. "Does Mr. Winterbourne think," she asked slowly, smiling, throwing back her head and glancing at him from head to foot, "that – to save my reputation – I ought to get into the carriage?"

Winterbourne coloured; for an instant he hesitated greatly. It seemed so strange to hear her speak that way of her "reputation." But he himself, in fact, must speak in accordance with gallantry. The finest gallantry, here, was simply to tell her the truth; and the truth, for Winterbourne, as the few indications I have been able to give have made him known to the reader, was that Daisy Miller should take Mrs. Walker's advice. He looked at her exquisite prettiness; and then he said very gently, "I think you should get into the carriage."

Daisy gave a violent laugh. "I never heard anything so stiff! If this is improper, Mrs. Walker," she pursued, "then I am all improper, and you must give me up. Good-by; I hope you'll have a lovely ride!" and, with Mr. Giovanelli, who made a triumphantly obsequious salute, she turned away.

Mrs. Walker sat looking after her, and there were tears in Mrs. Walker's eyes. "Get in here, sir," she said to Winterbourne, indicating the place beside her. The young man answered that he felt bound to accompany Miss Miller; whereupon Mrs. Walker declared that if he refused her this favour she would never speak to him again. She was evidently in earnest. Winterbourne overtook Daisy and her companion, and, offering the young girl his hand, told her that Mrs. Walker had made an imperious claim upon his society. He expected that in answer she would say something rather free, something to commit herself still further to that "recklessness" from which Mrs. Walker had so charitably endeavoured to dissuade her. But she only shook his hand, hardly looking at him; while Mr. Giovanelli bade him farewell with a too-emphatic flourish of the hat.

Winterbourne was not in the best possible humour as he took his seat in Mrs. Walker's victoria. "That was not clever of you," he said candidly, while the vehicle mingled again with the throng of carriages.

"In such a case," his companion answered, "I don't wish to be clever, I wish to be *earnest!*"

"Well, your earnestness has only offended her and put her off."

"It has happened very well," said Mrs. Walker. "If she is so perfectly determined to compromise herself, the sooner one knows it the better; one can act accordingly."

"I suspect she meant no harm," Winterbourne rejoined.

"So I thought a month ago. But she has been going too far."

"What has she been doing?"

"Everything that is not done here. Flirting with any man she could pick up; sitting in corners with mysterious Italians; dancing all the evening with the same partners; receiving visits at eleven o'clock at night. Her mother goes away when visitors come."

"But her brother," said Winterbourne, laughing, "sits up till midnight."

"He must be edified by what he sees. I'm told that at their hotel every one is talking about her, and that a smile goes round among all the servants when a gentleman comes and asks for Miss Miller."

"The servants be hanged!" said Winterbourne angrily. "The poor girl's only fault," he presently added, "is that she is very uncultivated."

"She is naturally indelicate," Mrs. Walker declared. "Take that example this morning. How long had you known her at Vevey?"

"A couple of days."

"Fancy, then, her making it a personal matter that you should have left the place!"

Winterbourne was silent for some moments, then he said, "I suspect, Mrs. Walker, that you and I have lived too long at Geneva!" And he added a request that she should inform him with what particular design she had made him enter her carriage.

"I wished to beg you to cease your relations with Miss Miller – not to flirt with her – to give her no further opportunity to expose herself – to let her alone, in short."

"I'm afraid I can't do that," said Winterbourne. "I like her extremely."

"All the more reason that you shouldn't help her to make a scandal."

"There shall be nothing scandalous in my attentions to her."

"There certainly will be in the way she takes them. But I have said what I had on my conscience," Mrs. Walker pursued. "If you wish to rejoin the young lady I will put you down. Here, by-the-way, you have a chance."

The carriage was traversing that part of the Pincian Garden that overhangs the wall of Rome and overlooks the beautiful Villa Borghese. It is bordered by a large parapet, near which there are several seats. One of the seats, at a distance, was occupied by a gentleman and a lady, towards whom Mrs. Walker gave a toss of her head. At the same moment these persons rose and walked towards the parapet. Winterbourne had asked the coachman to stop; he now descended from the carriage. His companion looked at him a moment in silence; then, while he raised his hat, she drove majestically away. Winterbourne stood there; he had turned his eyes towards Daisy and her cavalier. They evidently saw no one; they were too deeply occupied with each other. When they reached the low garden-wall they stood a moment looking off at the great flat-topped pine clusters of the Villa Borghese; then Giovanelli seated himself, familiarly, upon the broad ledge of the wall. The western sun in the opposite sky sent out a brilliant shaft through a couple of cloud-bars, whereupon Daisy's companion took her parasol out of her hands and opened it. She came a little nearer and he held the parasol over her; then, still holding it, he let it rest upon her shoulder, so that both of their heads were hidden from Winterbourne. This young man lingered a moment, then he began to walk. But he walked – not towards the couple with the parasol; towards the residence of his aunt, Mrs. Costello.

He flattered himself on the following day that there was no smiling among the servants when he, at least, asked for Mrs. Miller at her hotel. This lady and her daughter, however, were not at home; and on the next day after, repeating his visit, Winterbourne again had the misfortune not to find them. Mrs. Walker's party took place on the evening of the third day, and in spite of the frigidity of his last interview with the hostess Winterbourne was among the guests. Mrs. Walker was one of those American ladies who, while residing abroad, make a point, in their own phrase, of studying European society; and she had on this occasion collected several specimens of her diversely-born fellow-mortals to serve, as it were, as textbooks. When Winterbourne arrived Daisy Miller was not there, but in a few moments he saw her mother come in alone, very shyly and ruefully. Mrs. Miller's hair above her exposed-looking temples was more frizzled than ever. As she approached Mrs. Walker, Winterbourne also drew near.

"You see I've come all alone," said poor Mrs. Miller. "I'm so frightened; I don't know what to do; it's the first time I've ever been to a party alone – especially in this country. I wanted to bring Randolph or Eugenio, or someone, but Daisy just pushed me off by myself. I ain't used to going round alone."

"And does not your daughter intend to favour us with her society?" demanded Mrs. Walker, impressively.

"Well, Daisy's all dressed," said Mrs. Miller, with that accent of the dispassionate, if not of the philosophic, historian with which she always recorded the current incidents of her daughter's career. "She got dressed on purpose before dinner. But she's got a friend of hers there; that gentleman – the Italian – that she wanted to bring. They've got going at the piano; it seems as if they couldn't leave off. Mr. Giovanelli sings splendidly. But I guess they'll come before very long," concluded Mrs. Miller hopefully.

"I'm sorry she should come – in that way," said Mrs. Walker.

"Well, I told her that there was no use in her getting dressed before dinner if she was going to wait three hours," responded Daisy's mamma. "I didn't see the use of her putting on such a dress as that to sit round with Mr. Giovanelli."

"This is most horrible!" said Mrs. Walker, turning away and addressing herself to Winterbourne. "*Elle s'affiche.*[39] It's her revenge for my having ventured to remonstrate with her. When she comes I shall not speak to her."

Daisy came after eleven o'clock, but she was not, on such an occasion, a young lady to wait to be spoken to. She rustled forward in radiant loveliness, smiling and chattering, carrying a large bouquet and attended by Mr. Giovanelli. Everyone stopped talking, and turned and looked at her. She came straight to Mrs. Walker. "I'm afraid you thought I never was coming, so I sent mother off to tell you. I wanted to make Mr. Giovanelli practise some things before he came; you know he sings beautifully, and I want you to ask him to sing. This is Mr. Giovanelli; you know I introduced him to you; he's got the most lovely voice and he knows the most charming set of songs. I made him go over them this evening, on purpose; we had the greatest time at the hotel." Of all this Daisy delivered herself with the sweetest, brightest audibleness, looking now at her hostess and now round the room, while she gave a series of little pats, round her shoulders, to the edges of her dress. "Is there anyone I know?" she asked.

"I think every one knows you!" said Mrs. Walker pregnantly, and she gave a very cursory greeting to Mr. Giovanelli. This gentleman bore himself gallantly. He smiled and bowed and showed his white teeth, he curled his moustaches and rolled his eyes, and performed all the proper functions of a handsome Italian at an evening party. He sang, very prettily, half-a-dozen songs, though Mrs. Walker afterwards declared that she had been quite unable to find out who asked him. It was apparently not Daisy who had given him his orders. Daisy sat at a distance from the piano, and though she had publicly, as it were, professed a high admiration for his singing, talked, not inaudibly, while it was going on.

39. *Elle s'affiche*: She flaunts or makes a display of herself (French).

"It's a pity these rooms are so small; we can't dance," she said to Winterbourne as if she had seen him five minutes before.

"I am not sorry we can't dance," Winterbourne answered; "I don't dance."

"Of course you don't dance; you're too stiff," said Miss Daisy. "I hope you enjoyed your drive with Mrs. Walker."

"No, I didn't enjoy it; I preferred walking with you."

"We paired off, that was much better," said Daisy. "But did you ever hear anything so cool as Mrs. Walker's wanting me to get into her carriage and drop poor Mr. Giovanelli, and under the pretext that it was proper? People have different ideas! It would have been most unkind; he had been talking about that walk for ten days."

"He should not have talked about it at all," said Winterbourne; "he would never have proposed to a young lady of this country to walk about the streets with him."

"About the streets?" cried Daisy, with her pretty stare. "Where then would he have proposed to her to walk? The Pincio is not the streets, either; and I, thank goodness, am not a young lady of this country. The young ladies of this country have a dreadfully poky time of it, so far as I can learn; I don't see why I should change my habits for *them.*"

"I am afraid your habits are those of a flirt," said Winterbourne gravely.

"Of course they are," she cried, giving him her little smiling stare again. "I'm a fearful, frightful flirt! Did you ever hear of a nice girl that was not? But I suppose you will tell me now that I am not a nice girl."

"You're a very nice girl, but I wish you would flirt with me and me only," said Winterbourne.

"Ah! thank you, thank you very much; you are the last man I should think of flirting with. As I have had the pleasure of informing you, you are too stiff."

"You say that too often," said Winterbourne.

Daisy gave a delighted laugh. "If I could have the sweet hope of making you angry, I should say it again."

"Don't do that; when I am angry I'm stiffer than ever. But if you won't flirt with me, do cease at least to flirt with your friend at the piano; they don't understand that sort of thing here."

"I thought they understood nothing else!" exclaimed Daisy.

"Not in young unmarried women."

"It seems to me much more proper in young unmarried women than in old married ones," Daisy declared.

"Well," said Winterbourne, "when you deal with natives you must go by the custom of the place. Flirting is a purely American custom; it doesn't exist here. So when you show yourself in public with Mr. Giovanelli and without your mother ——"

"Gracious! poor mother!" interposed Daisy.

"Though you may be flirting, Mr. Giovanelli is not; he means something else."

"He isn't preaching, at any rate," said Daisy with vivacity. "And if you want very much to know, we are neither of us flirting, we are too good friends for that; we are very intimate friends."

"Ah!" rejoined Winterbourne, "if you are in love with each other it is another affair."

She had allowed him up to this point to talk so frankly that he had no expectation of shocking her by this ejaculation; but she immediately got up, blushing visibly, and leaving him to exclaim mentally that little American flirts were the queerest creatures in the world. "Mr. Giovanelli, at least," she said, giving her interlocutor a single glance, "never says such very disagreeable things to me."

Winterbourne was bewildered; he stood staring. Mr. Giovanelli had finished singing; he left the piano and came over to Daisy. "Won't you come into the other room and have some tea?" he asked, bending before her with his ornamental smile.

Daisy turned to Winterbourne, beginning to smile again. He was still more perplexed, for this inconsequent smile made nothing clear, though it seemed to prove, indeed, that she had a sweetness and softness that reverted instinctively to the pardon of offenses. "It has never occurred to Mr. Winterbourne to offer me any tea," she said, with her little tormenting manner.

"I have offered you advice," Winterbourne rejoined.

"I prefer weak tea!" cried Daisy, and she went off with the brilliant Giovanelli. She sat with him in the adjoining room, in the embrasure of the window, for the rest of the evening. There was an interesting performance at the piano, but neither of these young people gave heed to it. When Daisy came to take leave of Mrs. Walker, this lady conscientiously repaired the weakness of which she had been guilty at the moment of the young girl's arrival. She turned her back straight upon Miss Miller and left her to depart with what grace she might. Winterbourne was standing near the door; he saw it all. Daisy turned very pale and looked at her mother, but Mrs. Miller was humbly unconscious of any violation of the usual social forms. She appeared, indeed, to have felt an incongruous impulse to draw attention to her own striking observance of them. "Good-night, Mrs. Walker," she said; "we've had a beautiful evening. You see if I let Daisy come to parties without me, I don't want her to go away without me." Daisy turned away, looking with a pale, grave face at the circle near the door; Winterbourne saw that, for the first moment, she was too much shocked and puzzled even for indignation. He on his side was greatly touched.

"That was very cruel," he said to Mrs. Walker.

"She never enters my drawing-room again," replied his hostess.

Since Winterbourne was not to meet her in Mrs. Walker's drawing-room, he went as often as possible to Mrs. Miller's hotel. The ladies were rarely at home, but when he found them the devoted Giovanelli was always present. Very often the brilliant little Roman was in the drawing-room with Daisy alone, Mrs. Miller being apparently constantly of the opinion that discretion is the better part of surveillance. Winterbourne noted, at first with surprise, that Daisy on these occasions was never embarrassed or annoyed by his own entrance; but he very presently began to feel that she had no more surprises for him; the unexpected in her behaviour was the only thing to expect. She showed no displeasure at her *tête-à-tête* with Giovanelli being interrupted; she could chatter as freshly and freely with two gentlemen as with one; there was always, in her conversation, the same odd mixture of audacity and puerility. Winterbourne remarked to himself that if she was seriously interested in Giovanelli it was very singular that she should not take more trouble to preserve the sanctity of their interviews, and he liked her the more for her innocent-looking indifference and her apparently inexhaustible good humour. He could hardly have said why, but she seemed to him a girl who would never be jealous. At the risk of exciting a somewhat derisive smile on the reader's part, I may affirm that with regard to the women who had hitherto interested him, it very often seemed Winterbourne among the possibilities that, given certain contingencies, he should be afraid – literally afraid – of these ladies; he had a pleasant sense that he should never be afraid of Daisy Miller. It must be added that this sentiment was not altogether flattering to Daisy; it was part of his conviction, or rather of his apprehension, that she would prove a very light young person.

But she was evidently very much interested in Giovanelli. She looked at him whenever he spoke; she was perpetually telling him to do this and to do that; she was constantly "chaffing" and abusing him. She appeared completely to have forgotten that Winterbourne had said anything to displease her at Mrs. Walker's little party. One Sunday afternoon, having gone to St. Peter's with his aunt, Winterbourne perceived Daisy strolling about the great church in company with the inevitable Giovanelli. Presently he pointed out the young girl and her cavalier to Mrs. Costello. This lady looked at them a moment through her eyeglass, and then she said:

"That's what makes you so pensive in these days, eh?"

"I had not the least idea I was pensive," said the young man.

"You are very much pre-occupied, you are thinking of something."

"And what is it," he asked, "that you accuse me of thinking of?"

"Of that young lady's – Miss Baker's, Miss Chandler's – what's her name? Miss Miller's intrigue with that little barber's block."

"Do you call it an intrigue," Winterbourne asked – "an affair that goes on with such peculiar publicity?"

"That's their folly," said Mrs. Costello, "it's not their merit."

"No," rejoined Winterbourne, with something of that pensiveness to which his aunt had alluded. "I don't believe that there is anything to be called an intrigue."

"I have heard a dozen people speak of it; they say she is quite carried away by him."

"They are certainly very intimate," said Winterbourne.

Mrs. Costello inspected the young couple again with her optical instrument. "He is very handsome. One easily sees how it is. She thinks him the most elegant man in the world, the finest gentleman. She has never seen anything like him; he is better even than the courier. It was the courier probably who introduced him, and if he succeeds in marrying the young lady, the courier will come in for a magnificent commission."

"I don't believe she thinks of marrying him," said Winterbourne, "and I don't believe he hopes to marry her."

"You may be very sure she thinks of nothing. She goes on from day to day, from hour to hour, as they did in the Golden Age. I can imagine nothing more vulgar. And at the same time," added Mrs. Costello, "depend upon it that she may tell you any moment that she is 'engaged.'"

"I think that is more than Giovanelli expects," said Winterbourne.

"Who is Giovanelli?"

"The little Italian. I have asked questions about him and learned something. He is apparently a perfectly respectable little man. I believe he is in a small way, a *cavaliere avvocato*.[40] But he doesn't move in what are

---

40. *cavaliere avvacato*: Gentleman lawyer (Italian).

called the first circles. I think it is really not absolutely impossible that the courier introduced him. He is evidently immensely charmed with Miss Miller. If she thinks him the finest gentleman in the world, he, on his side, has never found himself in personal contact with such splendour, such opulence, such expensiveness, as this young lady's. And then she must seem to him wonderfully pretty and interesting. I rather doubt that he dreams of marrying her. That must appear to him too impossible a piece of luck. He has nothing but his handsome face to offer, and there is a substantial Mr. Miller in that mysterious land of dollars. Giovanelli knows that he hasn't a title to offer. If he were only a count or a *marchese*![41] He must wonder at his luck at the way they have taken him up."

"He accounts for it by his handsome face, and thinks Miss Miller a young lady *qui se passe ses fantaisies*!"[42] said Mrs. Costello.

"It is very true," Winterbourne pursued, "that Daisy and her mamma have not yet risen to that stage of – what shall I call it? – of culture, at which the idea of catching a count or a *marchese* begins. I believe that they are intellectually incapable of that conception."

"Ah! but the *avvocato* can't believe it," said Mrs. Costello.

Of the observation excited by Daisy's "intrigue," Winterbourne gathered that day at St. Peter's sufficient evidence. A dozen of the American colonists in Rome came to talk with Mrs. Costello, who sat on a little portable stool at the base of one of the great pilasters. The vesper service was going forward in splendid chants and organ-tones in the adjacent choir, and meanwhile, between Mrs. Costello and her friends, there was a great deal said about poor little Miss Miller's going really "too far." Winterbourne was not pleased with what he heard; but when, coming out upon the great steps of the church, he saw Daisy, who had emerged before him, get into an open cab with her accomplice and roll away through the cynical streets of Rome, he could not deny to himself that she was going very far indeed. He felt very sorry for her – not exactly that he believed that she had completely lost her head, but because it was painful to hear so much that was pretty, and undefended, and natural, assigned to a vulgar place among the categories of disorder. He made an attempt after this to give a hint to Mrs. Miller. He met one day in the Corso[43] a friend – a tourist like himself – who had just come out of the Doria Palace, where he had been walking

41. *marchese*: Nobleman (Italian).
42. *qui se passe ses fantaisies*: Who is indulging herself (French).
43. *Corso*: Via del Corso, a principal Roman boulevard.

through the beautiful gallery. His friend talked for a moment about the superb portrait of Innocent X by Velasquez,[44] which hangs in one of the cabinets of the palace, and then said, "And in the same cabinet, by-the-way, I had the pleasure of contemplating a picture of a different kind – that pretty American girl whom you pointed out to me last week." In answer to Winterbourne's inquiries, his friend narrated that the pretty American girl – prettier than ever – was seated with a companion in the secluded nook in which the great papal portrait was enshrined.

"Who was her companion?" asked Winterbourne.

"A little Italian with a bouquet in his button hole. The girl is delightfully pretty, but I thought I understood from you the other day that she was a young lady *du meilleur monde*."[45]

"So she is!" answered Winterbourne; and having assured himself that his informant had seen Daisy and her companion but five minutes before, he jumped into a cab and went to call on Mrs. Miller. She was at home; but she apologised to him for receiving him in Daisy's absence.

"She's gone out somewhere with Mr. Giovanelli," said Mrs. Miller. "She's always going round with Mr. Giovanelli."

"I have noticed that they are very intimate," Winterbourne observed.

"Oh! it seems as if they couldn't live without each other!" said Mrs. Miller. "Well, he's a real gentleman anyhow. I keep telling Daisy she's engaged!"

"And what does Daisy say?"

"Oh, she says she isn't engaged. But she might as well be!" this impartial parent resumed. "She goes on as if she was. But I've made Mr. Giovanelli promise to tell me, if *she* doesn't. I should want to write to Mr. Miller about it – shouldn't you?"

Winterbourne replied that he certainly should; and the state of mind of Daisy's mamma struck him as so unprecedented in the annals of parental vigilance that he gave up as utterly irrelevant the attempt to place her upon her guard.

After this Daisy was never at home, and Winterbourne ceased to meet her at the houses of their common acquaintance, because, as he perceived, these shrewd people had quite made up their minds that she was going too far. They ceased to invite her, and they intimated that they desired to express to observant Europeans the great truth that, though Miss Daisy

44. *Velasquez*: Diego Valázquez (1559–1660), Spanish Baroque painter.
45. *du meilleur monde*: Of the better society (French).

Miller was a young American lady, her behaviour was not representative – was regarded by her compatriots as abnormal. Winterbourne wondered how she felt about all the cold shoulders that were turned towards her, and sometimes it annoyed him to suspect that she did not feel at all. He said to himself that she was too light and childish, too uncultivated and unreasoning, too provincial, to have reflected upon her ostracism or even to have perceived it. Then at other moments he believed that she carried about in her elegant and irresponsible little organism a defiant, passionate, perfectly observant consciousness of the impression she produced. He asked himself whether Daisy's defiance came from the consciousness of innocence or from her being, essentially a young person of the reckless class. It must be admitted that holding oneself to a belief in Daisy's "innocence" came to seem to Winterbourne more and more a matter of fine-spun gallantry. As I have already had occasion to relate, he was angry at finding himself reduced to chopping logic about this young lady; he was vexed at his want of instinctive certitude as to how far her eccentricities were generic, national, and how far they were personal. From either view of them he had somehow missed her, and now it was too late. She was "carried away" by Mr. Giovanelli.

A few days after his brief interview with her mother, he encountered her in that beautiful abode of flowering desolation known as the Palace of the Cæsars. The early Roman spring had filled the air with bloom and perfume, and the rugged surface of the Palatine was muffled with tender verdure. Daisy was strolling along the top of one of those great mounds of ruin that are embanked with mossy marble and paved with monumental inscriptions. It seemed to him that Rome had never been so lovely as just then. He stood looking off at the enchanting harmony of line and colour that remotely encircles the city, inhaling the softly humid odours, and feeling the freshness of the year and the antiquity of the place reaffirm themselves in mysterious interfusion. It seemed to him also that Daisy had never looked so pretty; but this had been an observation of his whenever he met her. Giovanelli was at her side, and Giovanelli, too, wore an aspect of even unwonted brilliancy.

"Well," said Daisy, "I should think you would be lonesome!"

"Lonesome?" asked Winterbourne.

"You are always going round by yourself. Can't you get anyone to walk with you?"

"I am not so fortunate," said Winterbourne, "as your companion."

Giovanelli, from the first, had treated Winterbourne with distinguished politeness; he listened with a deferential air to his remarks; he laughed, punctiliously, at his pleasantries; he seemed disposed to testify to his belief that Winterbourne was a superior young man. He carried himself in no degree like a jealous wooer; he had obviously a great deal of tact; he had no objection to your expecting a little humility of him. It even seemed to Winterbourne at times that Giovanelli would find a certain mental relief in being able to have a private understanding with him – to say to him, as an intelligent man, that, bless you, *he* knew how extraordinary was this young lady, and didn't flatter himself with delusive – or at least *too* delusive – hopes of matrimony and dollars. On this occasion he strolled away from his companion to pluck a sprig of almond-blossom, which he carefully arranged in his button-hole.

"I know why you say that," said Daisy, watching Giovanelli. "Because you think I go round too much with *him*!" And she nodded at her attendant.

"Every one thinks so – if you care to know," said Winterbourne.

"Of course I care to know!" Daisy exclaimed seriously. "But I don't believe it. They are only pretending to be shocked. They don't really care a straw what I do. Besides, I don't go round so much."

"I think you will find they do care. They will show it – disagreeably."

Daisy looked at him a moment. "How – disagreeably?"

"Haven't you noticed anything?" Winterbourne asked.

"I have noticed you. But I noticed you were as stiff as an umbrella the first time I saw you."

"You will find I am not so stiff as several others," said Winterbourne, smiling.

"How shall I find it?"

"By going to see the others."

"What will they do to me?"

"They will give you the cold shoulder. Do you know what that means?"

Daisy was looking at him intently; she began to colour. "Do you mean as Mrs. Walker did the other night?"

"Exactly!" said Winterbourne.

She looked away at Giovanelli, who was decorating himself with his almond-blossom. Then looking back at Winterbourne – "I shouldn't think you would let people be so unkind!" she said.

"How can I help it?" he asked.

"I should think you would say something."

"I do say something;" and he paused a moment. "I say that your mother tells me that she believes you are engaged."

"Well, she does," said Daisy very simply.

Winterbourne began to laugh. "And does Randolph believe it?" he asked.

"I guess Randolph doesn't believe anything," said Daisy. Randolph's skepticism excited Winterbourne to further hilarity, and he observed that Giovanelli was coming back to them. Daisy, observing it too, addressed herself again to her countryman. "Since you have mentioned it," she said, "I *am* engaged." . . . Winterbourne looked at her; he had stopped laughing. "You don't believe it!" she added.

He was silent a moment; and then, "Yes, I believe it!" he said.

"Oh, no, you don't," she answered. "Well, then – I am not!"

The young girl and her cicerone[46] were on their way to the gate of the enclosure, so that Winterbourne, who had but lately entered, presently took leave of them. A week afterwards he went to dine at a beautiful villa on the Cælian Hill, and, on arriving, dismissed his hired vehicle. The evening was charming, and he promised himself the satisfaction of walking home beneath the Arch of Constantine and past the vaguely-lighted monuments of the Forum. There was a waning moon in the sky, and her radiance was not brilliant, but she was veiled in a thin cloud-curtain which seemed to diffuse and equalise it. When, on his return from the villa (it was eleven o'clock), Winterbourne approached the dusky circle of the Colosseum, it recurred to him, as a lover of the picturesque, that the interior, in the pale moonshine, would be well worth a glance. He turned aside and walked to one of the empty arches, near which, as he observed, an open carriage – one of the little Roman street-cabs – was stationed. Then he passed in, among the cavernous shadows of the great structure, and emerged upon the clear and silent arena. The place had never seemed to him more impressive. One-half of the gigantic circus was in deep shade; the other was sleeping in the luminous dusk. As he stood there he began to murmur Byron's famous lines, out of "Manfred"; but before he had finished his quotation he remembered that if nocturnal meditations in the Colosseum are recommended by the poets, they are deprecated by the doctors. The historic atmosphere was there, certainly; but the historic atmosphere, scientifically considered, was no better than a villainous miasma.[47] Winterbourne walked to the middle of the arena, to take a more general glance, intending thereafter to make a hasty retreat. The great cross in the center was covered with shadow; it was only as he drew near it that he made it out dis-

---

46. *cicerone:* Museum or sightseeing guide; here used ironically.
47. *miasma:* Stagnant air formerly associated with disease. See note 35.

tinctly. Then he saw that two persons were stationed upon the low steps which formed its base. One of these was a woman, seated; her companion was standing in front of her.

Presently the sound of the woman's voice came to him distinctly in the warm night-air. "Well, he looks at us as one of the old lions or tigers may have looked at the Christian martyrs!" These were the words he heard, in the familiar accent of Miss Daisy Miller.

"Let us hope he is not very hungry," responded the ingenious Giovanelli. "He will have to take me first; you will serve for dessert!"

Winterbourne stopped, with a sort of horror; and, it must be added, with a sort of relief. It was as if a sudden illumination had been flashed upon the ambiguity of Daisy's behaviour and the riddle had become easy to read. She was a young lady whom a gentleman need no longer be at pains to respect. He stood there looking at her – looking at her companion, and not reflecting that though he saw them vaguely, he himself must have been more brightly visible. He felt angry with himself that he had bothered so much about the right way of regarding Miss Daisy Miller. Then, as he was going to advance again, he checked himself; not from the fear that he was doing her injustice, but from a sense of the danger of appearing unbecomingly exhilarated by this sudden revulsion from cautious criticism. He turned away towards the entrance of the place; but as he did so he heard Daisy speak again.

"Why, it was Mr. Winterbourne! He saw me – and he cuts me!"

What a clever little reprobate she was, and how smartly she played at injured innocence! But he wouldn't cut her. Winterbourne came forward again, and went towards the great cross. Daisy had got up; Giovanelli lifted his hat. Winterbourne had now begun to think simply of the craziness, from a sanitary point of view, of a delicate young girl lounging away the evening in this nest of malaria. What if she *were* a clever little reprobate? that was no reason for her dying of the *perniciosa*.[48] "How long have you been here?" he asked, almost brutally.

Daisy, lovely in the flattering moonlight, looked at him a moment. Then – "All the evening," she answered, gently. . . . "I never saw anything so pretty."

"I am afraid," said Winterbourne, "that you will not think Roman fever very pretty. This is the way people catch it. I wonder," he added, turning

48. *perniciosa*: That is, Roman fever (Italian).

to Giovanelli, "that you, a native Roman, should countenance such a terrible indiscretion."

"Ah," said the handsome native, "for myself, I am not afraid."

"Neither am I — for you! I am speaking for this young lady."

Giovanelli lifted his well-shaped eyebrows and showed his brilliant teeth. But he took Winterbourne's rebuke with docility. "I told the Signorina it was a grave indiscretion; but when was the Signorina ever prudent?"

"I never was sick, and I don't mean to be!" the Signorina declared. "I don't look like much, but I'm healthy! I was bound to see the Colosseum by moonlight; I shouldn't have wanted to go home without that; and we have had the most beautiful time, haven't we, Mr. Giovanelli? If there has been any danger, Eugenio can give me some pills. He has got some splendid pills."

"I should advise you," said Winterbourne, "to drive home as fast as possible and take one!"

"What you say is very wise," Giovanelli rejoined. "I will go and make sure the carriage is at hand." And he went forward rapidly.

Daisy followed with Winterbourne. He kept looking at her; she seemed not in the least embarrassed. Winterbourne said nothing; Daisy chattered about the beauty of the place. "Well, I *have* seen the Colosseum by moonlight!" she exclaimed. "That's one good thing." Then, noticing Winterbourne's silence, she asked him why he didn't speak. He made no answer; he only began to laugh. They passed under one of the dark archways; Giovanelli was in front with the carriage. Here Daisy stopped a moment, looking at the young American. "*Did* you believe I was engaged the other day?" she asked.

"It doesn't matter what I believed the other day," said Winterbourne, still laughing.

"Well, what do you believe now?"

"I believe that it makes very little difference whether you are engaged or not!"

He felt the young girl's pretty eyes fixed upon him through the thick gloom of the archway; she was apparently going to answer. But Giovanelli hurried her forward. "Quick, quick," he said; "if we get in by midnight we are quite safe."

Daisy took her seat in the carriage, and the fortunate Italian placed himself beside her. "Don't forget Eugenio's pills!" said Winterbourne, as he lifted his hat.

"I don't care," said Daisy, in a little strange tone, "whether I have Roman fever or not!" Upon this the cab-driver cracked his whip, and they rolled away over the desultory patches of the antique pavement.

Winterbourne – to do him justice, as it were – mentioned to no one that he had encountered Miss Miller, at midnight, in the Colosseum with a gentleman; but nevertheless, a couple of days later, the fact of her having been there under these circumstances was known to every member of the little American circle, and commented accordingly. Winterbourne reflected that they had of course known it at the hotel, and that, after Daisy's return, there had been an exchange of remarks between the porter and the cab-driver. But the young man was conscious at the same moment that it had ceased to be a matter of serious regret to him that the little American flirt should be "talked about" by low-minded menials. These people, a day or two later, had serious information to give: the little American flirt was alarmingly ill. Winterbourne, when the rumour came to him, immediately went to the hotel for more news. He found that two or three charitable friends had preceded him, and that they were being entertained in Mrs. Miller's salon by Randolph.

"It's going round at night," said Randolph – "that's what made her sick. She's always going round at night. I shouldn't think she'd want to – it's so plaguey dark. You can't see anything here at night, except when there's a moon. In America there's always a moon!" Mrs. Miller was invisible; she was now, at least, giving her daughter the advantage of her society. It was evident that Daisy was dangerously ill.

Winterbourne went often to ask for news of her, and once he saw Mrs. Miller, who, though deeply alarmed, was – rather to his surprise – perfectly composed, and, as it appeared, a most efficient and judicious nurse. She talked a good deal about Dr. Davis, but Winterbourne paid her the compliment of saying to himself that she was not, after all, such a monstrous goose. "Daisy spoke of you the other day," she said to him. "Half the time she doesn't know what she's saying, but that time I think she did. She gave me a message; she told me to tell you. She told me to tell you that she never was engaged to that handsome Italian. I am sure I am very glad; Mr. Giovanelli hasn't been near us since she was taken ill. I thought he was so much of a gentleman; but I don't call that very polite! A lady told me that he was afraid I was angry with him for taking Daisy round at night. Well, so I am; but I suppose he knows I'm a lady. I would scorn to scold him. Any way, she says she's not engaged. I don't know why she wanted you to know; but she said to me three times – 'Mind you tell Mr. Winterbourne.' And then she told me to ask if you remembered the time you went to that castle, in Switzerland. But I said I wouldn't give any such messages as that. Only, if she is not engaged, I'm sure I'm glad to know it."

But, as Winterbourne had said, it mattered very little. A week after this the poor girl died; it had been a terrible case of the fever. Daisy's grave was in the little Protestant cemetery, in an angle of the wall of imperial Rome, beneath the cypresses and the thick spring-flowers. Winterbourne stood there beside it, with a number of other mourners; a number larger than the scandal excited by the young lady's career would have led you to expect. Near him stood Giovanelli, who came nearer still before Winterbourne turned away. Giovanelli was very pale; on this occasion he had no flower in his button-hole; he seemed to wish to say something. At last he said, "She was the most beautiful young lady I ever saw, and the most amiable." And then he added in a moment, "And she was the most innocent."

Winterbourne looked at him, and presently repeated his words, "And the most innocent?"

"The most innocent!"

Winterbourne felt sore and angry. "Why the devil," he asked, "did you take her to that fatal place?"

Mr. Giovanelli's urbanity was apparently imperturbable. He looked on the ground a moment, and then he said, "For myself, I had no fear; and she wanted to go."

"That was no reason!" Winterbourne declared.

The subtle Roman again dropped his eyes. "If she had lived, I should have got nothing. She would never have married me, I am sure."

"She would never have married you?"

"For a moment I hoped so. But no. I am sure."

Winterbourne listened to him; he stood staring at the raw protuberance among the April daisies. When he turned away again, Mr. Giovanelli, with his light slow step, had retired.

Winterbourne almost immediately left Rome; but the following summer he again met his aunt, Mrs. Costello, at Vevey. Mrs. Costello was fond of Vevey. In the interval Winterbourne had often thought of Daisy Miller and her mystifying manners. One day he spoke of her to his aunt – said it was on his conscience that he had done her injustice.

"I am sure I don't know," said Mrs. Costello. "How did your injustice affect her?"

"She sent me a message before her death which I didn't understand at the time. But I have understood it since. She would have appreciated one's esteem."

"Is that a modest way," asked Mrs. Costello, "of saying that she would have reciprocated one's affection?"

Winterbourne offered no answer to this question; but he presently said, "You were right in that remark that you made last summer. I was booked to make a mistake. I have lived too long in foreign parts."

Nevertheless, he went back to live at Geneva, whence there continue to come the most contradictory accounts of his motives of sojourn: a report that he is "studying" hard – an intimation that he is much interested in a very clever foreign lady.

Suggestions for Further Reading and Research

BIOGRAPHY

A PROLIFIC AUTHOR who zealously guarded his private life, James has proven to be an intriguing but elusive subject of biography. Simon Nowell-Smith, *The Legend of the Master* (London: Constable, 1947), and F. O. Matthiessen, *The James Family* (New York: Knopf, 1947), compile documents relevant to the biographical pursuit of James and the James family. Leon Edel's five-volume *Henry James* (Philadelphia: Lippincott, 1953-1972) marks the first massive treatment of the novelist's life; volumes 1 and 2, *Henry James: The Untried Years, 1843-1870* (1953) and *Henry James: The Conquest of London, 1870-1881* (1962), are particularly helpful for tracking the genesis, publication, and success of *Daisy Miller*. Kenneth Graham, *Henry James: A Literary Life* (New York: St. Martin's, 1995), focuses almost exclusively on James's development as a literary artist. Fred Kaplan, *Henry James: The Imagination of Genius—A Biography* (New York: Morrow, 1992), questions Edel's thesis that James maintained a rigorously celibate existence and inquires directly into the sexual and more specifically homoerotic dimensions of James's life. Sheldon M. Novick's controversial *Henry James: The Young Master* (New York: Random,

1996) and *Henry James: The Mature Master* (New York: Random, 2007) go further in this vein.

James authored a large body of nonfiction (travelogue, memoir, letters) and in so doing made himself the subject of autobiography. His travel writing has been reissued in two volumes: *Collected Travel Writing: English Hours, The American Scene, Other Travels*, edited by Richard Howard (New York: Library of America, 1993), and *Collected Travel Writing: The Continent*, edited by Richard Howard (New York: Library of America, 1993). His two late memoirs, *A Small Boy and Others* (1913) and *Notes of a Son and Brother* (1914), recall childhood and youth in the context of his remarkable family. Edited by Leon Edel, the four-volume *Henry James Letters*, 1843-1916 (Cambridge: Belknap P of Harvard UP, 1974-1984), offers James's own detailed epistolary documentation of his life in the moving present tense. A new comprehensive edition of James's letters edited by Pierre Walker and Greg W. Zacharias is in preparation; volume 1, *The Complete Letters of Henry James, 1855-1872* (Lincoln: U of Nebraska P, 2006), was published to considerable acclaim. James's own literary criticism along with the prefaces he wrote for the *New York Edition of Henry James* (1907-1909) have much to say about how he regarded his vocation as a novelist, his views with regard to the proper objectives of realist fiction, and the process by which particular narratives came to be composed. These writings (among them "Preface to 'Daisy Miller' &c.") are collected in *Henry James: Literary Criticism: French Writers; Other European Writers; The Prefaces to the New York Edition*, edited by Leon Edel and Mark Wilson (New York: Library of America, 1984).

CONTEXTS

Henry James's long, prolific, and international career compels the student to approach his life and work through multiple contextual frames: the James family; post-Civil War literary realism and the evolving market for journals and books; the rapid industrialization of the United States and its emergence as a global geopolitical player; the movement toward gender equality; the development of middle-class and upper-middle-class affluence and consumerism; grand-tour consumerism among old- and new-wealth demographics; and American expatriate communities. *The Cambridge Companion to Henry James*, edited by Jonathan Freedman (New York: Cambridge UP, 1998), and *Henry James in Context*, edited by David McWhirter (New York: Cambridge UP, 2010), are excellent starting points for readers who wish to see James and his work as products of the volatile late nineteenth and early twentieth centuries.

In recent years the literature of travel (fiction as well as nonfiction) has received increasing scholarly and theoretical attention and Henry James has emerged as a major figure in American travel-writing traditions. For a broad survey of these traditions, see Alfred Bendixen, "American Travel Books about Europe before the Civil War," and William Merrill Decker, "Americans in Europe from Henry James to the Present," in *The Cambridge Companion to American Travel*

Writing, edited by Alfred Bendixen and Judith Hamera (Cambridge: Cambridge UP, 2009); James Buzard, *The Beaten Track: European Tourism, Literature, and the Ways to "Culture" 1800–1918* (Oxford: Clarendon, 1993); and William W. Stowe, *Going Abroad: European Travel in Nineteenth-Century American Culture* (Princeton: Princeton UP, 1994). Jeremy Black's *The British Abroad: The Grand Tour in the Eighteenth Century* (London: History Press, 2003) and *Italy and the Grand Tour* (New Haven and London: Yale UP, 2003) provide rich historical accounts of the British travel patterns that shaped those of the United States. Lynne Withey, *Grand Tours and Cook's Tours: A History of Leisure Travel, 1750 to 1915* (New York: Morrow, 1997), documents the rise of international tourism as a British and American consumer industry. Roslyn Jolly, "Travel and Tourism" (*Henry James in Context*), addresses these themes as they appear in *Daisy Miller* and *The Wings of the Dove*.

CRITICAL STUDIES

Reflecting his phenomenal productivity as well as the enduring interest in his work, the body of critical writing about Henry James is vast. Accordingly the titles listed here should be understood as points of departure and by no means as an exhaustive list of the essential texts of James scholarship.

For readers coming to James for the first time, essay collections such as *The Cambridge Companion to Henry James*, edited by Jonathan Freedman (New York: Cambridge UP, 1998), and *Henry James in Context*, edited by David McWhirter (New York: Cambridge UP, 2010), showcase the vitality and diversity of critical response to the James oeuvre. *Daisy Miller* in such collections is discussed among a multitude of James titles, but its frequent mention underscores the novella's relevance to an understanding of the work that precedes and follows it. Daniel Mark Fogel's *Daisy Miller: A Dark Comedy of Manners* (Boston: Twayne, 1990) is particularly helpful to the novice student of James.

More advanced, comprehensive, and specialized pursuit of Henry James and his universe of themes will benefit from the following texts: Paul B. Armstrong, *The Phenomenology of Henry James* (Chapel Hill, U of North Carolina P, 1983); Millicent Bell, *Meaning in Henry James* (Cambridge: Harvard UP, 1991); Sharon Cameron, *Thinking in Henry James* (Chicago: U of Chicago P, 1989); Jonathan Freedman, *Professions of Taste: Henry James, British Aestheticism, and Commodity Culture* (Stanford: Stanford UP, 1990); Alfred Habegger, *Henry James and the "Woman Business"* (New York: Cambridge UP, 1989); Philip Horne, *Henry James and Revision* (New York: Oxford UP, 1990); Daniel Mark Fogel, *Henry James and the Structure of the Romantic Imagination* (Baton Rouge: LSU, 1981); Robert B. Pippen, *Henry James and Modern Moral Life* (New York: Cambridge UP, 2000); Ross Posnock, *The Trial of Curiosity: Henry James, William James, and the Challenge of Modernity* (New York: Oxford UP, 1991); Julie Rivkin, *False Positions: The Representational Logics of James's Fiction* (Stanford: Stanford UP, 1996); John Carlos Rowe, *The Theoretical Dimensions of Henry James* (Madison: U of Wisconsin P, 1984); Richard Salmon, *Henry James and the Culture of Publicity* (New York: Cambridge

UP, 1998); Hugh Stevens, *Henry James and Sexuality* (New York: Cambridge UP, 1998); and William Veeder, *Henry James—The Lessons of the Master: Popular Fiction and Personal Style in the Nineteenth Century* (Chicago: U of Chicago P, 1975).

Daisy Miller has been the focus of the following recent articles: Lisa Johnson's "Daisy Miller: Cowboy Feminist" (*Henry James Review* 22.1 [2001]: 41-58) and "'If This Is Improper, . . . Then I Am All Improper, and You Must Give Me Up': *Daisy Miller* and Other Uppity White Women as Resistant Emblems of America" in *Women as Sites of Culture: Women's Roles in Cultural Formation from the Renaissance to the Twentieth Century* (Aldershot, Eng.: Ashgate, 2002); Jeffrey Meyers, "'Daisy Miller' and the Romantic Poets" (*The Henry James Review* 28.1 [2007]: 94-100); George Monteiro, "What's in a Name? James' 'Daisy Miller'" (*American Literary Realism* 39.3 [2007]: 252-53); Dennis Pahl, "'Going Down' with Henry James's Uptown Girl: Genteel Anxiety and the Promiscuous World of Daisy Miller" (*Lit: Literature Interpretation Theory* 12.2 [2001]): 129-64); Penelope Pether, "Regarding the Miller Girls: Daisy, Judith, and the Seeming Paradox of in Re Grand Jury Subpoena in Judith Miller" (*Law and Literature* 19.2 [2007]: 187-206); Graham Smith, "'Latent Preparedness': Literary Association and Visual Reminiscence in 'Daisy Miller'" in *Illustrations, Optics and Objects in Nineteenth-Century Literary and Visual Culture* (Basingstoke, Eng.: Palgrave Macmillan, 2010); Adam Sonstegard, "Discreetly Depicting 'an Outrage': Graphic Illustration and 'Daisy Miller's Reputation" (*Henry James Review* 29.1 [2008]: 65-79); Sarah A. Wadsworth, "Innocence Abroad: Henry James and the Re-Invention of the American Woman Abroad" (*Henry James Review* 22.2 [2001]: 107-27); Lauren Weiner, "Tocquevillian Americans: Henry James, Daisy Miller, Pandora Day," in *Seers and Judges: American Literature as Political Philosophy* (Lanham: Lexington, 2002); Robert Weisbuch, "James and the American Sacred" (*Henry James Review* 22.3 [2001]; and William A. Wortman, "The 'Interminable Dramatic Daisy Miller'" (*Henry James Review* 28.3 [2007]: 281-91).

INTERNET SITES

The Henry James Society: This site reflects ongoing scholarly activity devoted to the life and works of Henry James, providing information on forthcoming conferences and an archive of papers presented at sessions sponsored by the Society. It also contains links to other sites of interest to students of James and his family. In addition to a website, the Society also maintains a Facebook page.

> http://mockingbird.creighton.edu/english/HJS/ElectronicArchives.html
> http://www.facebook.com/pages/Henry-James-Society-Inc/108679542508090

The Henry James Scholar's Guide to Web Sites: This site provides links to numerous etexts of Henry James's writings, major and minor, as well as to all issues of *The Henry James E-Journal* and other resources of interest to the student of James.

> http://www2.newpaltz.edu/~hathaway/

Glossary of Literary Terms

Abstract language Any language that employs intangible, nonspecific concepts. *Love, truth,* and *beauty* are abstractions. Abstract language is the opposite of concrete language. Both types have different effects and are important features of an author's style.

Allegory A narrative in which persons, objects, settings, or events represent general concepts, moral qualities, or other abstractions.

Antagonist A character in some fiction, whose motives and actions work against, or are thought to work against, those of the hero, or protagonist. The conflict between these characters shapes the plot of their story.

Archetype A term introduced in the 1930s by psychologist C. G. Jung, who described archetypes as "primordial images" repeated throughout human history. Archetypes, or archetypal patterns, recur in myths, religion, dreams, fantasies, and art, and are said to have power because we know them, even if unconsciously. In literature, archetypes appear in character types, plot patterns, and descriptions.

Characterization Characterization means the development of a character or characters throughout a story. Characterization includes the narrator's description of what characters look like and what they think, say, and do (these are sometimes very dissimilar). Their own actions and views of themselves, and other characters' views of and behavior toward them, are also means of characterization.

Characters One of the elements of fiction, characters are usually the people of a work of literature; characters may be animals or some other beings. Characters are those about whom a story is told and sometimes, too, the ones telling the story. Characters may be minor or major, depending on their importance to a story.

Climax The moment of greatest intensity and conflict in the action of a story is its climax.

Concrete language Any specific, physical language that appeals to one or more of the senses – sight, hearing, taste, smell, or touch. *Stones, chairs,* and *hands* are concrete words. Concrete language is the opposite of abstract language. Both types are important features of an author's style.

Conflict Antagonism between characters, ideas, or lines of action; between one character and the outside world; or between aspects of a character's own nature. Conflict is essential in a traditional plot.

Description Language that presents specific features of a character, object, or setting, or the details of an action or event.

Dialogue Words spoken by characters, often in the form of conversation between two or more. In stories and other forms of prose, dialogue is commonly enclosed between quotation marks. Dialogue is an important element in characterization and plot.

Diction A writer's selection of words. Particular patterns or arrangements of words in sentences and paragraphs constitute prose style. Hemingway's diction is said to be precise, concrete, and economical.

Didactic fiction A kind of fiction that is designed to present or demonstrate a moral, religious, political, or other belief or position. Didactic works are different from purely imaginative ones, which are written for their inherent interest and value. The distinction between imaginative and didactic writing is not always sharp.

Elements of fiction Major elements of fiction are plot, characters, setting, point of view, style, and theme. Skillful employment of these entities is essential in effective novels and stories. From beginning to end, each element is active and relates to the others dynamically.

Epiphany In literature, epiphany describes a sudden illumination of the significance or true meaning of a person, place, thing, idea, or situation. Often a word, gesture, or other action reveals the significance. The term was popularized by James Joyce, who explained it fully in his autobiographical novel *Stephen Hero* (written in 1914; pub. 1944).

Fiction Traditionally, a prose narrative whose plot, characters, and settings are constructions of its writer's imagination, which draws on his or her experiences and reflections. Short stories are comparatively short works of fiction, novels long ones.

Figurative language Suggestive, rather than literal, language employing metaphor, simile, or other figures of speech.

First-person narrator See **point of view**.

Flashback A writer's way of introducing important earlier material. As a narrator tells a story, he or she may stop the flow of events and direct the reader to an earlier time. Sometimes the reader is returned to the present, sometimes kept in the past.

Foreshadowing Words, gestures, and other actions that suggest future events or outcomes. An example would be a character saying, "I've got a bad feeling about this," and later in the narration something "bad" does happen to the character.

Genre A type or form of literature. The major literary genres are fiction, drama, poetry, and exposition (essay or book-length biography, criticism, history, and so on). Subgenres of fiction are the novel and the short story.

Image A word or group of words evoking concrete visual, auditory, or tactile associations. An image, sometimes called a "word-picture," is an important instance of figurative language.

Interior monologue An extended speech or narrative, presumed to be thought rather than spoken by a character. Interior monologues are similar to, but different from, *stream of consciousness*, which describes mental life at the border of consciousness. Interior monologues are typically more consciously controlled and conventionally structured, however private their thoughts.

Irony A way of writing or speaking that asserts the opposite of what the author, reader, and character know to be true. *Verbal* or *rhetorical* irony accomplishes these contradictory meanings by direct misstatements. *Situational* irony is achieved when events in a narrative turn out to be very different from, or even opposite to, what is expected.

Narrative A narrator's story of characters and events over a period of time. Usually the characters can be analyzed and generally understood; usually the events proceed in a cause-and-effect relation; and usually some unity can be found among the characters, plot, point of view, style, and theme of a narrative. Novels as well as stories are usually narratives, and journalism commonly employs narrative form.

Narrator The storyteller, usually an observer who is narrating in the *third-person point of view*, or a participant in the story's action speaking in the first person. Style and tone are important clues to the nature of a narrator and the validity and objectivity of the story itself. Sometimes a narrator who takes part in the action is too emotionally involved to be trusted for objectivity or accuracy. This narrator would be called an *unreliable narrator.*

Naturalism A literary movement that began in France in the late nineteenth century, spread, moderated, and influenced much twentieth-century literature. The movement, which started in reaction against the antiscientific sentimentality of the period, borrowed from the principles, aims, and methods of scientific thinkers such as Darwin and Spencer. Early naturalists held that human lives are determined externally by society and internally by drives and instincts and that free will is an illusion. Writers were to proceed in a reporterlike, objective manner. Stephen Crane shows the influence of early naturalism, Ernest Hemingway of later, more moderate, naturalism.

Novel An extended prose narrative or work of prose fiction, usually published alone. Hawthorne's *The Scarlet Letter* is a fairly short novel, Melville's *Moby-Dick, or, the Whale* a very long one. The length of a novel enables its author to develop characters, plot, and settings in greater detail than a short story writer can.

Novella Between the short story and the novel in size and complexity. Like them, the novella is a work of prose fiction. Sometimes it is called a long short story.

Omniscient narrator See **point of view.**

Parable A simple story that illustrates a moral point or teaches a lesson. The persons, places, things, and events are connected by the moral question only. The moral position of a parable is developed through the choices of people who believe and act in certain ways and are not abstract personifications as in allegory, nor animal characters as in folktales.

Parody Usually, a comic or satirical imitation of a serious piece of writing, exaggerating its weaknesses and ignoring its strengths. Its distinctive features are ridiculed through exaggeration and inappropriate placement in the parody.

Plot One of the elements of fiction, plot is the sequence of major events in a story, usually in a cause-effect relation. Plot and character are intimately related, since characters carry out the plot's action. Plots may be described as simple or complex, depending on their degree of complication. "Traditional" writers usually plot their stories tightly; modernist writers employ looser, often ambiguous plots.

Point of view One of the elements of fiction, point of view is the perspective, or angle of vision, from which a narrator presents a story. Point of view tells us about the narrator as well as about the characters, setting, and theme of a story. Two common points of view are *first-person narration* and *third-person narration.* If a narrator speaks of himself or herself as "I," the narration is in the first person; if the narrator's self is not apparent and the story is told about others from some distance, using "he," "she," "it," and "they," then third-person narration is likely in force. The point of view may be *omniscient* (all-knowing) or *limited.* When determining a story's point of view, it is helpful to decide whether the narrator is reporting events as they are happening or as they happened in the past; is observing or participating in the action; and is or is not emotionally involved.

Protagonist The hero or main character of a narrative or drama. The action is the presentation and resolution of the protagonist's conflict, internal or external; if the conflict is with another major character, that character is the antagonist.

Realism Literature that seeks to present life as it is really lived by real people, without didacticism or moral agendas. In the eighteenth and nineteenth centuries realism was controversial; today it is usual.

Regionalism Literature that is strongly identified with a specific place. Writers like Kate Chopin who concentrate on one area are called regional realists; writers who do so for several works are said to have strong regional elements in their body of work.

Rising action The part of a story's action that develops its conflict and leads to its climax.

Setting One of the elements of fiction, setting is the context for the action: the time, place, culture, and atmosphere in which it occurs. A work may have several settings; the relation among them may be significant to the meaning of the work.

Short story A short work of narrative fiction whose plot, characters, settings, point of view, style, and theme reinforce each other, often in subtle ways, creating an overall unity.

Stream of consciousness A narrative technique primarily based on the works of psychologist-philosophers Sigmund Freud, Henri Bergson, and William James, who originated the phrase in 1890. In fiction, the technique is designed to represent a character's inner thoughts, which flow in a stream without grammatical structure and punctuation or apparent coherence. The novels *Ulysses* and *Finnegans Wake*, by James Joyce, contain the most famous and celebrated use of the technique. Stream of consciousness, which represents the borders of consciousness, may be distinguished from the *interior monologue*, which is more structured and rational.

Structure The organizational pattern or relation among the parts of a story. Questions to help determine a story's structure may include the following: Is the story told without stop from beginning to end, or is it divided into sections? Does the narrator begin at the beginning of a plot, or when actions are already under way (*in medias res*, in the middle of things)?

Does the narrator begin at the end of the plot and tell the story through a series of flashbacks? Is the story organized by major events or episodes, or by images or moods?

Style One of the elements of fiction, style in a literary work refers to the diction (choice of words), syntax (arrangement of words), and other linguistic features of a work. Just as no two people have identical fingerprints or voices, so no two writers use words in exactly the same way. Style distinguishes one writer's language from another's.

Symbol A reference to a concrete image, object, character, pattern, or action whose associations evoke significant meanings beyond the literal ones. An *archetype*, or archetypal symbol, is a symbol whose associations are said to be universal — that is, they extend beyond the locale of a particular nation or culture. Religious symbols, such as the cross, are of this kind. In literature, *symbolism* refers to an author's use of symbols.

Theme One of the elements of fiction, the theme is the main idea that is explored in a story. Characters, plot, settings, point of view, and style all contribute to a theme's development.

Third-person narrator See **point of view.**

Tone Like tone of voice. Literary tone is determined by the attitude of a narrator toward characters in a story and the story's readers. For example, the tone of a work may be impassioned, playful, haughty, grim, or matter-of-fact. Tone is distinct from atmosphere, which refers to the mood of a story and can be analyzed as part of its setting.

Unity The oneness of a short story. Generally, each of a story's elements has a unity of its own, and all reinforce each other to create an overall unity. Although a story's unity may be evident on first reading, much more often discovering the unity requires rereading, reflection, and analysis. Readers who engage themselves in these ways experience the pleasure of bringing a story to life.

About the Editor

WILLIAM MERRILL DECKER (Ph.D., University of Iowa) is professor of English at Oklahoma State University. He is the author of *The Literary Vocation of Henry Adams* (1990), *Epistolary Practices: Letter Writing in America before Telecommunications* (1998), and *Kodak Elegy: A Cold War Childhood* (2012). He is an editor of and contributor to *Henry Adams and the Need to Know* (2005) and has authored essays that appear in *The Cambridge Companion to American Travel Writing* (2009), *Hearts of Darkness: Melville, Conrad, and Narratives of Oppression* (2010), and *Leather-Stocking Redux; or, Old Tales, New Essays* (2011). The recipient of Fulbright and DAAD fellowships, he has taught at universities in Belgium and Germany. He serves on the editorial board of *The Bedford Anthology of American Literature*.